John Bonenperger
4243 Williamsburg Dr. Apt. C
Harrisburg, PA 17109

BASEBALL'S TOP 100

KERRY BANKS

Baseball's

TOP 100

THE GAME'S
GREATEST RECORDS

GREYSTONE BOOKS

D&M PUBLISHING INC.

Vancouver/Toronto/Berkeley

*To my brother Brian, who I struck out
hundreds of times with my wiffle curve.*

Greystone Books
An imprint of D&M Publishers Inc.
2323 Quebec Street, Suite 201
Vancouver BC Canada V5T 4S7
www.greystonebooks.com

*Library and Archives Canada
Cataloguing in Publication*
Banks, Kerry, 1952–
Baseball's top 100 : the game's greatest
records / Kerry Banks.
Includes index.
ISBN 978-1-55365-507-7
1. Baseball—Miscellanea. I. Title.

GV873.B235 2010 796.357 C2009-905383-7

Editing by Derek Fairbridge
Cover design by Peter Cocking
Typesetting by Naomi MacDougall
Cover illustration © Tom Schierlitz/
Stone/Getty Images
For a complete list of photo credits see p. 156
Printed and bound in China by
C&C Offset Printing Co., Ltd.
Printed on acid-free paper
Distributed in the U.S. by Publishers Group West

We gratefully acknowledge the financial support
of the Canada Council for the Arts, the British
Columbia Arts Council, the Province of British
Columbia through the Book Publishing Tax Credit
and the Government of Canada through the Book
Publishing Industry Development Program (BPIDP)
for our publishing activities.

INTRODUCTION

You hold in your hands a dangerous book. Not dangerous for you; dangerous for me. Baseball, more than any other sport, reveres its records and its record holders, which makes writing a book like this a dicey enterprise. Debate is inevitable. Simply selecting which 100 baseball records to include was a challenge in itself, but to take the next step and rank them in order of importance was a real mind-bender. There is no magic formula to all of this, no sabermetric gymnastics one can perform to arrive at bulletproof answers. Strict objectivity is impossible. However, there are several criteria that I employed as guidelines: the historical importance of a record, its longevity, its margin of domination, its likelihood of being surpassed and its level of difficulty were all taken into consideration.

In choosing the records, I tried to avoid those that would fall under the title of "fantastic feats." So stuff like Ed Reulbach's 1906 iron-man feat of pitching two complete-game shutouts in a doubleheader and Fernando Tatis's freakish feat of clubbing two grand slams in one inning in 1999 are not included. Also missing is Bobo Holloman's feat of pitching a no-hitter for the St. Louis Browns in his first start on May 6, 1953. Amazing? Certainly, especially since it was the only complete game that Holloman tossed in his entire major-league career, but not exactly a record.

I also steered clear of including records set before 1901, when the majors became a two-league organization. Players accomplished some remarkable things in the early years of baseball, but the rules were quite different. Hoss Radbourn won 59 games and struck out 441 batters for the National League's Providence Grays in 1884. And he did it in a 112-game schedule! Of course, the mound was only 50 feet from the plate and you needed six balls to get a walk. That was also the first year that overhand pitching was allowed. In 1887, Tip O'Neill batted .485 for the American Association's St. Louis Browns, but then bases on balls were counted as hits that year.

You will find Barry Bonds's name attached to several records in the book. Because of his difficult personality and his association with steroids, Bonds may be the most unpopular superstar in baseball history. But whether you like him or not, he still holds a number of prestigious records. In fact, many of baseball's biggest records are now owned by suspected, or in some cases, confirmed cheaters. Besides Bonds, the roster of rogues includes Roger Clemens, Alex Rodriguez, Éric Gagné and Manny Ramirez. Of course, hundreds of other modern-day players have also tried to elevate their game with a chemical boost. If you scan the list of the majors' top 25 home-run hitters in 2001, the season that Bonds put 73 homers into orbit, you will find that virtually all of them have been accused or proven to have used some type of performance-enhancing drugs. If Bonds was on the juice, he was certainly not alone.

There are also several record holders in the book whose names may not be familiar, such as Ray Grimes, Chief Wilson, Jack Taylor and Earl Webb. Yet, they all hold significant records, and so this a welcome opportunity to shine a light on their overlooked exploits. On the flip side, some Hall of Famers who one would expect to see in a book like this, do not appear. For example, Honus Wagner, Sandy Koufax, Roberto Clemente, George Brett and Mike Schmidt may have all posted amazing stats, but they own very few records, and none of them managed to find a spot in my top 100.

But enough with the preamble; let's start at the top.

Kerry Banks
September 2009

MOST CONSECUTIVE GAMES WITH A HIT

56: Joe DiMaggio, New York Yankees, May 15 to July 16, 1941

The streak of streaks began without fanfare on May 15, 1941. On that day, Joltin' Joe DiMaggio went one-for-four against pitcher Eddie Smith and the Chicago White Sox. It did not end until a hot night in mid-July when Cleveland pitchers Al Smith and Jim Bagby Jr., aided by two outstanding fielding plays by third baseman Ken Keltner, brought an end to DiMaggio's 56-game hitting tear. Besides defying the laws of probability and captivating the nation, the streak also had a major impact on the pennant race. When it started, the Yankees had a 14–15 record and were 6.5 games behind in the American League pennant race. When it ended, they were 55–37 and solidly on top. During his streak DiMaggio had 22 multi-hit games, batted a torrid .408, cracked 15 homers, scored 56 runs and drove in 55. Incredibly, with the streak over, he began a new one. The Yankee Clipper rapped hits in the next 16 consecutive games—giving him the distinction of having hit safely in 72 of 73 games. Such sustained excellence eludes most mortals, and it is what makes DiMaggio's record so tough to break. There is scant margin for error, with one off night able to spoil the chase. Since 1941, Pete Rose is the only player to come remotely close to matching the feat, hitting safely in 44 straight games in 1978.

MOST HOME RUNS, CAREER

762: Barry Bonds, 1986 to 2007

Crack! On August 7, 2007, Barry Bonds broke Hank Aaron's career record of 755 home runs by smashing a full-count, 85-mph pitch from Washington's Mike Bacsik deep into the California night. Bonds surpassed the revered milestone at San Francisco's AT&T Park, maybe the only place where he knew the cheers would outnumber the jeers from those who accused him of steroid use. Besides the psychological and physical traits associated with steroid use, such as anger issues and the bulked-up physique and enlarged head that Bonds displayed later in his career, he also appeared to defy Father Time. To overtake Aaron, the Giants slugger had to hit a miraculous 311 home runs after turning 35, an age when most players' skills and power are waning. In 1999, at age 34, Bonds had only 445 four-baggers, but he proceeded to thump 258 in the next five seasons, an average of 52 per year. This was a major increase over the 186 homers he collected in the previous five years, when he averaged 37 per year. While the controversy that surrounds Bonds has tainted his record of 762 round-trippers, he is not likely to match Aaron's 31-year reign as baseball's home-run king. Alex Rodriguez, still a relatively youthful 34, and unlike Bonds an admitted former steroid-user, is on pace to surpass Bonds's record within the next five years.

HIGHEST BATTING AVERAGE, CAREER

.366: Ty Cobb, 1905 to 1928

Playing baseball with an aggressiveness that often verged on the homi-
cidal and brawling with teammates, opposing players, team employees
and even fans, Ty Cobb was not an easy man to like. Still, one can't
help but admire his awesome hitting numbers. His .366 lifetime batting
average is untouchable. Only 12 players in the last 50 years have posted
a higher average in a single season than Cobb managed over his 24-year
career. That average was for many years believed to be .367, but when
researchers discovered a mistake, his average was corrected to .366. The
outfielder batted over .370 a total of 11 times, hit over .400 three times,
and won 11 batting titles with the Detroit Tigers. Cobb was rarely recognized for his power, but he led the AL in slugging average eight times.
In later life, he sneered at the new breed of power hitters, claiming that
he could have hit a bunch of home runs if he had wanted to, but that he
preferred a more scientific approach to the game. On May 5, 1925, the
38-year-old outfielder blasted three homers in one game, reputedly to
prove to reporters that he was indeed serious about this boast. Although
Babe Ruth is now widely regarded as the greatest of the old-time players,
when the two were inducted into the Hall of Fame in 1936, it was Cobb
who received the most votes in the balloting.

4

MOST HOME RUNS, ONE SEASON

73: Barry Bonds, San Francisco Giants, 2001

Let's assume that Barry Bonds was on the juice when he cranked 73 long flies over the fences in 2001. We are still looking at a colossal feat. The Giants' kingpin had only 476 official at-bats that year in 153 games, largely because terrified opposing teams walked him a record-setting 177 times. He averaged one home run for every 6.5 at-bats, establishing yet another major-league record, as Bonds's onslaught eclipsed Mark McGwire's 70-homer effort in 1998 and his average of one round-tripper for every 7.3 at-bats. Bonds belted number 71 off Chan Ho Park in the first inning of a game against the Dodgers on October 5. It came on his first swing since hitting number 70 at Houston's Enron Field off rookie Wilfredo Rodriguez the night before. After smashing a 442-foot shot into the bleachers, an elated Bonds circled the bases and was mobbed at the plate by his teammates and his 11-year-old son, Nikolai. In a moment of serendipity, his historic homer came at the same time that McGwire was approaching the plate at Busch Stadium in St. Louis, where the Cards were playing Houston. The 'Frisco slugger went yard again off Park two innings later. He finished up the season with one more circuit clout two days later, leaving the new record at 73. At age 36, Bonds became the oldest player to lead either league in dingers.

MOST HITS, CAREER

4,256: Pete Rose, 1963 to 1986

Pete Rose was an overrated player in his heyday (Joe Morgan and Johnny Bench were better all-around players on Cincy's Big Red Machine), and even Rose admitted, "There are a lot of better players than me, but I do the same thing day in and day out, year in and year out." Yet in retirement, Rose has become underrated, his exploits diminished by his lifetime suspension for gambling and his prison stint for tax evasion. But make no mistake about it: Rose was a terrific hitter. He batted .300 or better 15 times and won four batting titles, the last at age 40. He had a record 10 seasons with 200 hits and led the National League in doubles five times. He also made the All-Star team in 17 seasons at five different positions. Still, it is Rose's career record for hits that ranks as his greatest distinction. To set the mark he had to chase down the legendary Ty Cobb and his total of 4,191. Rose passed Cobb with his 4,192nd hit, a single off Padres pitcher Eric Show on September 11, 1985. Or did he? Independent research has revealed that two of Cobb's hits were counted twice. Because of this, it's now thought that Rose actually broke Cobb's record against the Cubs' Reggie Patterson with a single in the first inning of a game on September 8. All told, Rose compiled 4,256 hits before his final at-bat, a strikeout against San Diego's Goose Gossage on August 17, 1986.

MOST NO-HITTERS, CAREER

7: Nolan Ryan, 1966 to 1993

Only five pitchers in history have thrown more than two no-hitters: Cy Young, Bob Feller and Larry Corcoran had three; Sandy Koufax had four; and Nolan Ryan had seven. That margin of domination in such an elite category says a lot about Ryan, whose 100-mph fastball put the fear in batters for 27 years. There was never another pitcher quite as intimidating or overpowering. Also, there was never another pitcher who threw so hard for so long. You can better appreciate Ryan's amazing longevity when you realize that he tossed his first no-hitter against the Kansas City Royals on May 15, 1973, and threw his last 18 years later, at age 44, against the Toronto Blue Jays on May 1, 1991. Despite his advanced age, it was one of Ryan's most masterful performances. Of his 122 pitches, 83 were strikes. The Jays hit only eight balls in fair territory all night; only four out of the infield. And the legendary hurler struck out 16 batters! His final victim was second baseman Robbie Alomar. Coincidentally, Robbie's father, Sandy Alomar Sr., had been the second baseman in each of Ryan's first two no-hitters. Of Ryan's seven no-hitters, four were pitched for California, one for Houston and two for Texas. With a little luck there could have been more: Ryan also pitched a record 12 complete-game one-hitters.

MOST CONSECUTIVE SCORELESS
INNINGS PITCHED, ONE SEASON

59: Orel Hershiser, Los Angeles Dodgers,
August 30 to September 29, 1988

They called him "Bulldog," not because the whippet-thin pitcher resembled one, but because of his tenacity and mental toughness. Those traits were on display for all to see in 1988 when Orel Hershiser won the NL Cy Young Award with a 23–8 record and 2.26 ERA. But it was in September that the sinkerballer took his game to a new level, tossing five complete-game shutouts to compile a string of 49 scoreless innings and close within nine innings of a record that seemed unbreakable: Don Drysdale's 58 innings of scoreless ball. Drysdale set his record with the Dodgers in 1968, twirling six consecutive shutouts. Hershiser needed to blank San Diego in his last start of the season to tie the record. As it turned out, Hershiser and Padres hurler Andy Hawkins waged a terrific battle, throwing shutouts through nine innings, thus giving Hershiser a shot at snaring the record in the 10th. Coincidentally, Drysdale, a Dodger broadcaster, was at the game, and after Hershiser blanked the Padres in the 10th, Drysdale went out to hug him and offer his congratulations. Incredibly, in the opener of the NLCS against the Mets, Hershiser hurled another eight and one-third scoreless innings before allowing a run, extending his miraculous streak to 67 innings.

MOST CONSECUTIVE GAMES PLAYED

2,632: Cal Ripken, Jr., May 30, 1982 to September 20, 1998

Lou Gehrig's iron-man record of 2,130 consecutive games played was supposed to be untouchable, at least until Cal Ripken Jr. came along. Ripken surpassed Gehrig's 56-year-old record when he played in his 2,131st game on September 6, 1995, a contest between the Baltimore Orioles and California Angels played in front of a sold-out crowd at Oriole Park at Camden Yards. To make the feat even more memorable, Ripken hit a home run in the previous night's game and another homer in his 2,131st game. When the game became official after the Angels' half of the fifth inning, the numerical banners on the wall of the B&O Warehouse outside the stadium's rightfield wall changed from 2,130 to 2,131. Everyone attending (including the Angels and all four umpires) erupted with a standing ovation that lasted more than 22 minutes. As applause rained down, Ripken did a lap around the warning track to shake hands and give high fives to the fans, creating a highlight-reel moment that has been replayed repeatedly in the ensuing years. The Orioles' 19-time All-Star played in an additional 502 straight games over the next three years, before his streak ended at 2,632 games when he voluntarily removed his name from the lineup on Baltimore's final home game in 1998.

MOST CONSECUTIVE WORLD SERIES TITLES

5: New York Yankees, 1949 to 1953

From 1921 to 1964, the New York Yankees won 29 pennants. Led by Lou Gehrig and Joe DiMaggio, they claimed four consecutive World Series titles from 1936 to 1939. But from 1949 to 1953, the Yanks did the unbelievable, capturing five straight World Series with machine-like precision, winning 20 of 28 Series games over that span. The streak began when Casey Stengel was hired as manager. His appointment was considered controversial, given that in his nine previous seasons as a bench boss in the majors, Stengel posted only one winning season, and had earned a reputation as a clown. Few predicted success, as New York had finished third the year before and looked to be in decline. But the Yanks had a solid pitching staff, featuring Vic Raschi, Allie Reynolds and Ed Lopat, and despite a rash of injuries, Stengel guided them to the pennant, overtaking Boston in the season's final two games. Although an influx of young talent strengthened the Yanks in subsequent years, only once in those five seasons—1953—did they win the AL pennant by more than five games. By the time New York had won its fifth straight Series, opinions of Stengel had changed. Said pitcher Don Larsen: "I don't think anybody could have managed our club like Casey did. He made what some people call stupid moves, but about eight or nine out of 10 of them worked."

HIGHEST SLUGGING AVERAGE, ONE SEASON

.863: Barry Bonds, San Francisco Giants, 2001

Slugging average, which is calculated by determining a batter's total bases and dividing that number by his official times at bat, provides a handy measure of a player's power. A slugging average of .700 is rare. Some of the game's greatest power hitters—Joe DiMaggio, Hank Aaron, Willie Mays—never registered a slugging average of .700 in even their best seasons. So an average over .800 (eight total bases for every 10 times at-bat) is practically unheard of. In fact, after more than a century of baseball, only one player—Babe Ruth—had ever topped the mark. In 1920 and 1921, the Yankee legend recorded booming averages of .849 and .846. But Barry Bonds turned back the tide of history in 2001 when he belted 73 homers and posted a supersonic .863 slugging average. The enigmatic Giants star achieved these gaudy stats despite being walked an incredible 177 times by opposing pitchers. Of his 156 hits, 47 percent left the ballpark. Was it a chemically enhanced performance? Quite likely. But then Bonds would certainly not be the only modern-day player who got a boost from a vial. In fact, virtually all of the 25 top home-run hitters in the majors in 2001 have since been accused of or admitted to using steroids. So why has no one else put up anything close to Bonds's numbers?

MOST WORLD SERIES WON BY A PLAYER

10: Yogi Berra, 1946 to 1965

Yogi Berra is remembered today more for his Yogisms—"This is like déjà vu all over again." "It ain't over till it's over."—than for his achievements on the field, which is a shame because Berra was one of the greats. In fact, in his 2001 *Historical Baseball Abstract*, Bill James tabbed Berra as the number-one catcher of all time, better than Johnny Bench, Roy Campanella and Mickey Cochrane. Although Berra would not have won 10 World Series titles and 14 AL pennants had he entered the majors at another time, or with a different team, his stellar catching, pitch-calling and clutch hitting were an integral part of the Yankees' success. Whitey Ford claimed he never shook off one of Berra's signs, and Don Larsen said the same thing after he tossed his World Series perfect game. Beginning in 1949, Berra led the Yanks in RBIs seven straight seasons—not bad on a team that had Joe DiMaggio and Mickey Mantle. During that seven-year run, the stubby catcher copped three MVP Awards (1951, 1954, 1955) and also finished second (1953), third (1950) and fourth (1952) in the voting. He made the All-Star team 14 years in a row and 15 times in total. Besides winning 10 World Series rings, Berra owns other Series records that should last forever, including games played (75), hits (71) and catcher putouts (457).

HIGHEST SLUGGING AVERAGE, CAREER

.690: Babe Ruth, 1914 to 1935

The old-timers claimed that when Babe Ruth connected, there was no mistaking the sound. "It was like two billiard balls crashing together," said one writer. Ruth's cannonading shots spelled an end to the deadball era and generated a buzz across America. His career slugging average of .690 leaves everyone else in the dust. Ted Williams ranks a distant second at .634, and aside from Albert Pujols, who is still early in his career, only five other players have posted career figures above .600. Even Barry Bonds stands a whopping 82 percentage points behind Ruth. Remarkably, the Babe sustained his power pace for most of a 22-year career, leading the American League in slugging 13 times. The Bambino's offensive blitz began after he was sold to the Yankees by the Boston Red Sox following the 1919 season. Eager to make an impression in the Big Apple, Ruth clubbed 54 homers, a total that exceeded every other *team* in the majors, except for the Philadelphia Phillies. That same season, Ruth slugged a colossal .849, a record that stood for more than 80 years. In 1920, the Yankees, coincidentally, became the first team to draw more than one million fans to a ballpark, more than double the attendance of any other club. As Yankee manager Miller Huggins observed, "They all flock to see him, because the American fan likes the fellow who carries the wallop."

LOWEST EARNED-RUN AVERAGE, ONE SEASON (MODERN-DAY)

1.12: Bob Gibson, St. Louis Cardinals, 1968

Yes, it's true that pitching monopolized baseball in 1968, and yes, it's true that two dead-ball era pitchers—Dutch Leonard and Mordecai "Three Finger" Brown—posted lower single-season ERAs than Bob Gibson, but Gibson's performance in 1968 still ranks as miraculous. His ERA was 1.12, which is a live-ball era record and the major-league record in 300 or more innings pitched. Throwing only a blazing fastball and a knee-buckling slider, Gibson made hitters look foolish time and again through power and guile. Opponents collectively batted a miserable .184 against him and had just a .233 on-base percentage. The glowering Cardinals ace racked up 268 strikeouts and 13 shutouts, second only to Grover Cleveland Alexander's 1916 record of 16, and during one incredible span from June 2 through July 30, he allowed only two earned runs in 92 straight innings. One runner scored on a wild pitch and the other on a bloop double that was fair by inches. Those were the only things standing between Gibson and 10 straight shutouts. The fiery hurler did post 47 consecutive scoreless innings, at the time the third-longest scoreless streak in major-league history. He also won the Cy Young and the MVP Award. And yet, somehow, despite his overpowering dominance, Gibson's win-loss record was only 22–9.

14

HIGHEST BATTING AVERAGE, ONE SEASON
(MODERN-DAY)

.406: Ted Williams, Boston Red Sox, 1941

The .406 batting average that Ted Williams posted in 1941 is not the highest of all time. Most fans would be hard-pressed to come up with that record and its holder: Hugh Duffy batted .440 in 1894. But Williams's number has a resounding echo. That's partly because time has shown how difficult a feat it truly was, but also because of the manner in which he accomplished it. The Red Sox star ended a day below .400 just 29 times—20 of them before a 4-for-5 day against New York on May 25 pumped his average to .404. Williams did not just get hot at the right time; he essentially had a 143-game hitting streak. He entered the last day of the 1941 season hitting .39955, which rounds off to .400. Manager Joe Cronin suggested Williams sit out Boston's doubleheader with the Athletics to preserve his .400 average. But Williams chose to play. In the first game he ripped a homer and three singles in five at-bats. In the nightcap, he had a double and a single in three at-bats. With his six hits on the day, the Splendid Splinter finished at .406. Interestingly, the sacrifice-fly rule was not in effect in 1941 (sacrifice flies were counted as at-bats). Had it been, Williams—who drove home six runners on fly balls during the season—would not have needed to perform his last-day heroics. He would have hit .411.

HIGHEST TEAM WINNING PERCENTAGE, ONE SEASON

.763: Chicago Cubs, 1906

The Chicago Cubs registered 116 wins and only 36 losses in 1906, but, due in large part to their disappointing performance in the World Series, the team is not remembered as one of the greatest of all time. Chicago's record-setting season was built on the arms of its stellar pitching staff. The Cubs led the majors with a team 1.76 ERA and six of the club's hurlers finished with double-digit victories: Mordecai "Three Finger" Brown (26), Jack Pfiester (20), Ed Reulbach (19), Carl Lundgren (17), Orvie Overall (12) and Jack Taylor (12). Brown also led all pitchers with a sterling 1.04 ERA, the lowest ever posted by a pitcher with at least 250 innings. For Brown, it was the start of a streak of six consecutive 20-win seasons for Chicago. The Cubs breezed to the NL pennant, finishing a whopping 20 games ahead of the second-place New York Giants, and might have actually finished with 118 wins, but were not allowed to make up two games that had been postponed. The Cubs went into the World Series as heavy favorites over their crosstown rivals, the White Sox, who won 93 games to capture the AL flag despite a dismal team batting average of .230. The teams split the first two games of the Series, but the Pale Hose unexpectedly exploded for 26 hits in the last two games, winning 8–6 and 8–3, to take the title.

MOST CONSECUTIVE BATTERS
RETIRED BY A PITCHER, ONE GAME

36: Harvey Haddix, Pittsburgh Pirates, May 26, 1959

Harvey Haddix had a head cold when he took the mound to face the Milwaukee Braves on a cool, misty night on May 26, 1959, at Milwaukee's County Stadium. Even without the congestion, the 33-year-old looked to be in for a tough outing against the defending NL champions and pitcher Lew Burdette. As it turned out, neither team could push across a run. "Every batter, it was zip, zip—two strikes," Haddix said in 1989, on the 30th anniversary of the game. "I've had a lot better stuff than that night, but I never had control like that." After nine innings the Pirates lefty had pitched a perfect game, throwing only 78 pitches, but the score was tied 0–0. Incredibly, the game continued into the 13th inning, still scoreless, with the two starters still in the game and with Haddix still perfect. Then, Milwaukee's leadoff batter, Felix Mantilla, reached first on an error and advanced to second on a sacrifice. Haddix intentionally walked Hank Aaron, and Joe Adcock followed with a home run for an apparent 3–0 victory, but Aaron mistakenly left the field and Adcock passed him on the basepaths. Both were called out, while Mantilla scored, making the final 1–0. Hard-luck Haddix was left with a one-hit loss after retiring 36 consecutive batters in what some consider the greatest pitching performance of all time.

MOST TOTAL BASES, CAREER

6,856: Hank Aaron, 1954 to 1976

Early in 1965, the Los Angeles Dodgers pitching staff was discussing strategies for handling the dangerous hitters they would face in the coming year: Frank Robinson, Willie Mays, Dick Allen, Willie McCovey. When they reached Hank Aaron's name the room fell silent. "Make sure," someone finally said, "there's no one on when he hits it out." Pitchers never did discover how to shut down the soft-spoken outfielder with the rattlesnake-quick wrists. Fastballs were the slugger's bread and butter. As Cardinals pitcher Curt Simmons noted, "Trying to throw a fastball by Henry Aaron is like trying to sneak a sunrise past a rooster." Aaron may have been underrated by fans because of his quiet and understated style, but not by the men who played against him. As Mickey Mantle noted in 1970: "As far as I'm concerned, Hank Aaron is the best ballplayer of my era. He is to baseball of the last 15 years what Joe DiMaggio was before him. He's never received the credit he's due." By the time he retired, Aaron had compiled 2,174 runs, 3,771 hits, 624 doubles, 98 triples, 755 home runs (a record that lasted 31 years) and a record 2,297 RBIs. His 6,856 total bases is 722 more than runner-up Stan Musial, a huge margin of domination, especially when you consider that the gap between Musial and 12th place Dave Winfield is only 713 total bases.

MOST STRIKEOUTS BY A PITCHER, CAREER

5,714: Nolan Ryan, 1966 to 1993

The 3,000-strikeout club is an elite fraternity. It has only 16 members. The 5,000-strikeout club is a kingdom unto itself, and there is only one member—Nolan Ryan. The next closest hurler is Randy Johnson with 4,875. For a pitcher to surpass Ryan's career record of 5,714 strikeouts, he would have to fan an average of 285 batters for 20 consecutive seasons. I think we can safely predict that it won't be done, at least not until the Commissioner's Office allows bionic arms. As Astros coach Matt Galante once noted: "People talk about records that won't be broken. Nolan's strikeout record is right near the top. You have to have the combination of high strikeout totals and longevity. Those are two things that don't often go together. To do what Nolan did and keep doing it for as long as he did—you won't see that again." Ryan's record-setting trail of strikeouts began with Atlanta Braves pitcher Pat Jarvis on September 11, 1966, and ended with California Angels catcher Greg Myers on September 17, 1993. Along the way, the rifle-armed Texan posted 10 or more strikeouts in a game 215 times. In 1973, while with the Angels, he struck out 10 or more batters a record 23 times. He had six seasons of 300 or more strikeouts, 15 seasons of 200 or more strikeouts, and 24 seasons of 100 or more strikeouts.

MOST STOLEN BASES, CAREER

1,406: Rickey Henderson, 1979 to 2003

Rickey Henderson was a man in motion from the very beginning—he was born on Christmas Day 1958 in the backseat of a '57 Olds en route to a Chicago hospital. (His father had been winning at a poker game and didn't want to leave). If speed kills, then Henderson was a mass murderer. He swiped a base in his big-league debut with Oakland and went on to lead his league in steals 12 times, the last at age 39. When Henderson broke Lou Brock's career mark of 938 steals on May 1, 1991, at Oakland Coliseum, there was a brief ceremony. With Brock standing next to him, Henderson modestly proclaimed, "Lou Brock was certainly a great base stealer, but today I'm the greatest of all time." It's hard to dispute his assessment. His career total is nearly 50 percent more than Brock's record; the 468-steal difference alone would place Henderson in the top 50 base stealers of all-time. But stealing was only part of the story. Henderson also collected 3,055 hits, scored a MLB record 2,295 runs and is second on the career walks list with 2,190. He hit 297 home runs, including 81 to lead off a game (another record), made 10 All-Star teams and won an MVP Award. "He was the most dangerous player of our generation," said Tony La Russa, a former manager of Henderson's. "That includes all the great sluggers and Hall of Famers. He was the most dangerous."

MOST SHUTOUTS, CAREER

110: Walter Johnson, 1907 to 1927

Ty Cobb once described the first time he and his Detroit Tiger team-mates faced Walter Johnson. "I watched him take that easy windup. And then something went past me that made me flinch. The thing just hissed with danger. We couldn't touch him . . . every one of us knew we'd met the most powerful arm ever turned loose in a ballpark." During a dazzling 21-year career, Johnson won 416 games and posted 20-win seasons a dozen times, including 10 in a row, and twice topped 30 wins (33 in 1912) and (36 in 1913). The numbers are even more impressive when you consider that he did this while pitching for the Washington Senators, a team that lived in the second division and didn't win a pennant until Johnson was 37. Riding high atop the right-hander's list of feats is his 110 shutouts, the most in baseball history. Johnson had a 38–26 record in games decided by a 1–0 score, and he lost 65 games in which his team failed to score a run. Until Nolan Ryan and Steve Carlton passed him in 1983, Johnson held the major-league mark of 3,500 strikeouts, racking them up almost exclusively with one pitch: a sidearm fastball. It was no surprise then that the Big Train joined Cobb, Babe Ruth, Honus Wagner and Christy Mathewson as one of the "Five Immortals" elected to Cooperstown in the first year of balloting.

21

HIGHEST ON-BASE PERCENTAGE, ONE SEASON

.609: Barry Bonds, San Francisco Giants, 2004

Even though on-base percentage (hits, plus walks and times hit by pitch, divided by at-bats) was developed in the late 1940s by Dodgers general manager Branch Rickey and statistician Allan Roth as a more accurate gauge of a batter's effectiveness than batting average, baseball was slow to accept this statistic. Today, we know better. Ted Williams's on-base percentage of .553, set in 1941, the year he hit .406, looked unassailable, but Barry Bonds made mincemeat of Williams's record, posting a .582 percentage in 2002, before belting it into another dimension with a .609 mark in 2004. Although the Bay Area bomber collected only 135 hits in 2004, he batted .362 with an astonishing 232 walks, 120 of which were intentional, which, when added to his nine times hit by a pitch, means Bonds reached base safely 376 times. Incredibly, this is not the all-time record; Babe Ruth reached base 379 times in 1923, albeit with 82 more plate appearances. Even so, to reach base six out of every 10 at-bats in a season, and to do it at age 40, is an eye-popping feat. Of course, it would not have happened if San Francisco had a bonafide power hitter to bat behind Bonds in the order. All year long opposing teams walked him with impunity—a major reason why the Giants finished two games behind the Dodgers in the NL West and one game back of Houston for the wild-card berth.

HIGHEST ON-BASE PERCENTAGE, CAREER

.482: Ted Williams, 1939 to 1960

In the spring of 2002, when Ben Cherrington and Theo Epstein took over the baseball operations for the Boston Red Sox, their first act was to hand out copies of Ted Williams's book *The Science of Hitting* to every player in the system. "He defines everything that we hope our organizational philosophy will follow," said Epstein. "Get a good pitch to hit" was the essence of Teddy Ballgame's philosophy, and no one did it better than Williams, who was disciplined at the plate and blessed with superb eyesight. The Red Sox slugger paced the AL in on-base percentage 12 times; five times he led the circuit by more than 50 points, something accomplished only eight other times in baseball history. Williams's .344 lifetime batting average is the highest of any player with 500 homers, and he was the last major leaguer to hit .400, reaching the milestone in 1941 when he batted .406. In total, he captured six batting crowns. Understandably, pitchers hated to see him standing in the batter's box. As lefty Bobby Shantz recalled: "Did they tell me how to pitch to Williams? Sure they did. It was great advice, very encouraging. They said he had no weakness, won't swing at a bad ball, has the best eyes in the business and can kill you with one swing. He won't hit anything bad, but don't give him anything good."

MOST RUNS BATTED IN, ONE SEASON

191: Hack Wilson, Chicago Cubs, 1930

From the waist up, Hack Wilson was built like a blacksmith, with a barrel chest and massive arms. But all that muscle was mounted on a stumpy pair of legs and tiny feet. Wilson stood only five foot six but weighed 190 pounds and had an 18-inch collar with size six shoes. A fan favorite, he was the NL's most feared slugger in the late 1920s. In 1930, with the Cubs, the 30-year-old outfielder had a monster season, batting .356 with a then NL-record 56 homers and a MLB-record 191 RBIS, undoubtedly aided by a ball that NL owners had juiced to unprecedented levels to boost offense and attendance. Wilson's RBI mark withstood challenges by Lou Gehrig (184) and Hank Greenberg (183), and today, 80 years later, the record looks more invincible than ever. Even during the steroid soaked era of the late 1990s and early 2000s, the nearest any player came to it was Manny Ramirez, who amassed 165 RBIS for Cleveland in 1999. Wilson himself never came remotely close to repeating his feat. In 1931, he clashed with newly hired manager Rogers Hornsby, began drinking heavily and saw his power numbers tumble. Out of baseball by 1935, he was reduced to handing out towels at a Baltimore pool, and he died of a pulmonary edema and sclerotic liver in 1948. Wilson was just 48.

24

LOWEST WHIP, ONE SEASON

0.74: Pedro Martinez, Boston Red Sox, 2000

Pedro Martinez's WHIP (the number of hits and walks allowed, divided by innings pitched) in 2000 was 0.74, not only breaking a 87-year-old modern major-league record of 0.78 set by Walter Johnson, but also the all-time mark of 0.77 set by Guy Hecker in 1882. In a year of superheated bats, AL hitters slugged a mere .259 against Martinez. He also limited opposition hitters to an anemic .167 batting average and .213 on-base percentage, both modern-day MLB records. The skinny Dominican became the only starting pitcher in history to amass more than twice as many strikeouts in a season (284) as hits allowed (128). Though his win-loss record was only 18–6, he posted a sterling 1.74 ERA, the AL's lowest since Ron Guidry's 1.74 in 1978, while copping his third Cy Young Award. His ERA was even more astounding when you realize that the league average was 5.07 that year. No other starting pitcher has ever had such a gigantic differential. In 1999 and 2000, Martinez allowed 288 hits, 597 strikeouts, 69 walks and a 1.90 ERA in 430 innings. Some statisticians believe that under the circumstances—with hitter-friendly Fenway Park as his home field, in a league with the designated hitter, during the steroid-soaked boom years—this two-year performance represents the peak for any pitcher in baseball history.

25

HIGHEST BATTING AVERAGE OVER A FIVE-YEAR SPAN

.402: Rogers Hornsby, St. Louis Cardinals, 1921 to 1925

Rogers Hornsby lived for baseball. The rest of life held little meaning. He wouldn't go to movies or read books for fear of ruining his batting eye. "People ask me what I do in winter when there's no baseball," Hornsby once said. "I'll tell you what I do. I stare out the window and wait for spring." The Texan's single-minded intensity helped him become the game's greatest right-handed hitter. From 1921 to 1925 with the Cardinals, "Rajah" won five NL batting titles, hitting .397, .401, .384, .424 and .403. Not even Ty Cobb ever compiled a five-year stretch in which he averaged over .400. And Hornsby also hit for power and racked up high on-base percentages. In 1922, he won the NL Triple Crown, leading the league in home runs (42), RBIs (152) and average (.401). Two years later, Hornsby hit an astounding .424, while leading the loop in hits, doubles, runs, walks, slugging and on-base percentage. Even so, he finished second in the MVP voting behind Brooklyn pitcher Dazzy Vance, who was 28–6, with 262 strikeouts and a 2.16 ERA. The voters likely spurned Hornsby due to his personality. One writer characterized him as "a liturgy of hatred." His main focus was winning, and he wasn't shy about criticizing anyone—teammates, opponents, managers and owners alike—whom he felt didn't share his will to win.

MOST CONSECUTIVE GAMES REACHING BASE SAFELY

84: Ted Williams, Boston Red Sox, July 1 to September 28, 1949

Although it remains one of Ted Williams's least-known records, his feat of reaching base in 84 straight games is arguably one of his most impressive achievements. In setting the standard, Williams surpassed Joe DiMaggio's 1941 record of 74 games, and his own single-season high of 69 straight games, also set in 1941. During the 1949 streak, which lasted more than half a season, Williams compiled a torrid on-base average of .593. His streak finally ended when Boston was edged 2–1 by Washington Senators pitcher Ray Scarborough. The Washington hurler struck out Williams twice and got him to fly out to center in his three plate appearances. Interestingly, Williams was in the on-deck circle when Johnny Pesky was retired for the third out in the top of the ninth. Despite setting the record and winning the MVP Award with a league-leading 43 home runs and 159 RBIs, Teddy Ballgame's season ended in frustration, as the Yankees beat the Red Sox in the season finale to cop the pennant. Williams, who went 0 for 2 in the final game, lost the batting title by 0.0002 to Detroit's George Kell, who hit .3429 to Williams's .3427. If Williams had had one more hit or one less at-bat that season, he would have become the only player to win the Triple Crown three times.

MOST RUNS SCORED, CAREER

2,295: Rickey Henderson, 1979 to 2003

There was no great hullabaloo when Rickey Henderson broke Ty Cobb's 73-year-old record for career runs by scoring number 2,246 on October 4, 2001. Baseball fans were more preoccupied with Barry Bonds's pursuit of Mark McGwire's single-season home-run record and the impending retirements of Cal Ripken Jr. and Tony Gwynn. Henderson celebrated the moment by sliding into home plate, even though he had just hit a homer. Despite the lack of public acclaim, this ranks as one of baseball's most prestigious records and the one that Henderson values the most of all his many achievements. As he noted, "You have to score to win." Reaching base and scoring runs any way possible are the prime objectives of a leadoff hitter, and Henderson did it better than anyone. To increase his chances of getting aboard by a walk, he batted in an exaggerated crouch, shrinking his strike zone, which sportswriter Jim Murray described as being "smaller than Hitler's heart." And once on base, he created havoc with his baserunning skills. Henderson plated more than 100 runs 13 times in his career. In 1985, with the Yankees, he logged 146 runs, the most since Ted Williams in 1950, and became the first player since Lou Gehrig in 1936 to amass more runs in a season than games played.

MOST CONSECUTIVE 200-HIT SEASONS, CAREER

9: Ichiro Suzuki, 2001 to 2009

"No power." "Can't pull the ball." "Too small." The North American critics had plenty to say about Ichiro Suzuki, much of it bad, after seeing him in action for the first time in the spring of 2001. Many predicted that Seattle's high-priced Japanese import would be a flop. Wow, were they ever wrong. Not only did Suzuki hit .350 to win the AL batting crown, he also ripped 242 hits to set a new major-league rookie record. Since then the hits have just kept coming. On September 13, 2009, in a contest against Texas, Ichiro beat out an infield roller to reach the 200-hit mark for the ninth consecutive season. With that single, the 35-year-old surpassed Wee Willie Keeler's standard of eight straight seasons with 200 hits, a record that had endured 108 years. Ichiro is now just one shy of Pete Rose's record total of 10 seasons with 200 hits. Even more amazing, Ichiro accomplished this in his first nine seasons in the majors. How tough is it to get 200 hits in a season? Pretty tough: it has only been done 470 times since 1901. Willie Mays reached the plateau just once, Joe DiMaggio twice, Babe Ruth three times. Doing it nine times in a row is downright spooky, although Ichiro is not the type to let it go to his head. "When I break a record, I never feel satisfaction," he said after the Texas game. "I always want to feel satisfaction, but when I accomplish a record, I only feel relief."

29

LONGEST WINNING STREAK BY A TEAM

26 games: New York Giants, September 7 to 30, 1916

There are numerous oddities connected with this record. One: the 1916 Giants were no powerhouse—only one of their regulars batted above .300 in 1916, and they had no 20-game winners. Two: the Giants had a 17-game winning streak earlier in the season and yet still finished fourth, seven games back of Brooklyn. Three: the Giants played 28½ games during the streak. There was a four-inning rainout, they beat the Yankees in an exhibition game, and played a 1–1 tie with Pittsburgh that was called after eight innings due to rain. (Because tie games were replayed back then, it didn't count as part of the permanent record.) Four: all the games in the streak, including nine doubleheaders, were played at the Polo Grounds. Five: manager John McGraw used the same lineup and batting order in all the games, except for the two catchers. The key to the streak was the club's starting pitching: using an array of spitters, curves and fastballs, with stellar control (33 walks in 245 innings), the staff turned in 22 complete games. The pitchers were aided by an airtight defense that played 15 errorless games and executed 15 double plays. The final stats for the streak? Giants: 122 runs, 229 hits, 19 errors; Brooklyn, Philadelphia, Cincinnati, Pittsburgh, Chicago, St. Louis, Boston: 33 runs, 146 hits, 53 errors.

MOST WINS, CAREER

511: Cy Young, 1890 to 1911

Cy Young's 511 wins are often cited as baseball's most unbreakable record. However, this does not make it the game's greatest record. Although it is difficult to evaluate the achievements of a player who began his big-league career pitching underhand from a mound that was five and a half feet closer to the plate, we can say a few things with certainty. Young's huge numbers are largely a product of his amazing durability and longevity, the fact he played on a lot of strong teams and also because had the good fortune to join the newly created American League in 1901, when baseball expanded from eight to 16 teams. Flourishing in this diluted talent pool, his victory total zoomed from 20 to a league-leading 33. Facing weaker hitters in the junior circuit, he won 226 games after the age of 33. It is worth noting that Young also holds "unbreakable" records for innings pitched (7,357), complete games (749) and losses (313). He had a record 15 seasons of 20 or more wins, and five seasons of 30 or more wins, but he led his league in victories only four times and only twice in ERA, and he averaged about a hit per inning, a formula for disaster in today's game. Even so, Young was a remarkable talent. If his namesake award had existed during his era, it's likely he would have won four of them.

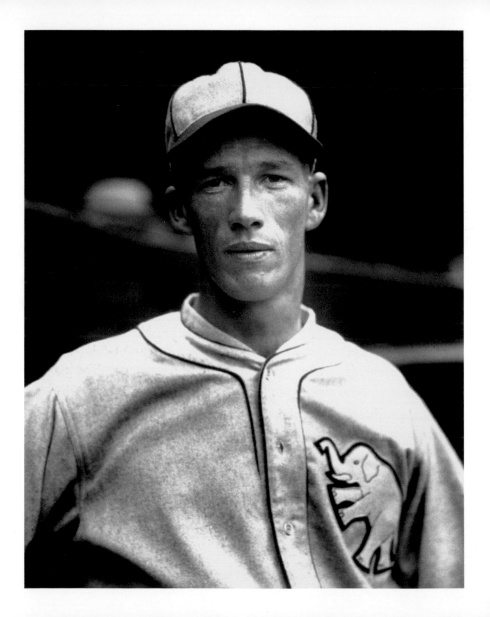

MOST EARNED-RUN AVERAGE TITLES, CAREER

9: Lefty Grove, 1926 to 1939

Lefty Grove's signature pitch was his fastball. "He could throw a lamb chop past a wolf," said sportswriter Arthur Baer. The son of a Maryland coal miner, Grove left school in eighth grade and worked in the mines and on railroad crews. He gained entry into baseball when word of his lively arm reached Jack Dunn, the man who discovered Babe Ruth and ran the Baltimore Orioles of the International League. Grove spent five years blowing away batters in Baltimore until Dunn finally sold his meal ticket to Connie Mack's Philadelphia A's for a record $100,600. The six-foot-three southpaw quickly became the club's marquee pitcher, posting mesmerizing numbers in a hitter-dominated era. Grove paced the AL in strikeouts for seven consecutive seasons from 1925 to 1931, and rang up seven straight 20-win seasons from 1927 to 1933. The hot-tempered flamethrower also led the league in winning percentage five times, as well as shredded uniforms and overturned water buckets. Yet perhaps the best indicator of Grove's excellence is his record nine ERA crowns. (No other pitcher has won more than five.) His 2.06 ERA for Philadelphia in 1931 was 2.32 runs below the league average, another AL record, and his lifetime ERA of 3.06, when adjusted for the ballparks and the hitting-happy era in which he played, is among the best of any pitcher in history.

MOST STOLEN BASES, ONE SEASON

130: Rickey Henderson, Oakland Athletics, 1982

Rickey Henderson broke into the big leagues with the Oakland A's in 1979, batting .274 with 33 stolen bases in 89 games. The next year, the A's hired Billy Martin to manage the team, and Martin's aggressive style helped catapult Henderson to superstardom. Martin encouraged the speedster to steal at will, and he took full advantage of the opportunity, swiping 100 bags in his first full season in 1980. In 1981, a strike-shortened season, he stole 56 bases in 108 games, and led the AL in hits. In 1982, Henderson set his aim on Lou Brock's single-season record of 118 stolen bases, set in 1974. Running at virtually every opportunity, the thick-thighed bandit swiped 49 bags in Oakland's first 50 games and had 84 by the All-Star break. On August 27, Henderson brazenly stole four bases in a 5–4 loss to Milwaukee to raise his total to 122 and break Brock's mark. The record-breaking 119th steal came off pitcher Doc Medich and catcher Ted Simmons on a third-inning pitchout. Henderson had 123 steals at the end of August, but with his body banged up from all the running he had done, he played in just 11 of Oakland's final 33 games, swiping only seven more bases, though he finished with a flourish, thieving three in the last game of the season to round out the record at a tidy 130.

MOST TOTAL BASES, ONE SEASON

457: Babe Ruth, New York Yankees, 1921

Babe Ruth had several extraordinary hitting seasons, which makes it very difficult to choose one as the best, but many baseball observers believe that 1921 was his finest campaign. In fact, it is often cited as the single best offensive season of all time. Ruth set major-league records for runs (177), extra-base hits (119) and total bases (457), and boasted an .846 slugging average—just three percentage points below his 1920 mark. Moreover, he batted .378, walked 144 times and drove in 171 runs, carrying the Yankees to their first pennant. Yet, as impressive as the Sultan of Swat's 1921 numbers were, they could have been more astounding under modern conditions. Bill Jenkinson's 2006 book, *The Year Babe Ruth hit 104 Home Runs*, examines each of Ruth's 714 career home runs, plus several hundred long inside-the-park drives and "fair-foul" balls. Until 1931 in the AL, any balls that hit the foul pole were considered ground-rule doubles, and balls that went over the wall in fair territory but hooked foul were ruled foul. Many fields, including Ruth's 1921 home, the Polo Grounds, had exceptionally deep center fields—in the Polo Grounds' case, nearly 500 feet. Jenkinson concluded that Ruth would have been credited with 104 home runs in 1921, if modern rules and field dimensions had been in place.

MOST CONSECUTIVE NO-HITTERS

2: Johnny Vander Meer, Cincinnati Reds, June 11, 15, 1938

Johnny Vander Meer compiled 29 shutouts in his 13-year career, but only two are remembered. On June 11, 1938, the southpaw tossed a no-hitter as the Reds beat the Boston Braves 3–0. Four days later, he faced the Brooklyn Dodgers in the first night game played at Ebbets Field. A crowd of 38,748, including Vander Meer's parents and 500 fans from his hometown of Prospect Park, New Jersey, attended the event. Vander Meer pitched brilliantly, holding Brooklyn hitless for eight innings as the Reds surged to a 6–0 lead. But in the ninth, his control suddenly deserted him. After retiring Buddy Hassett on a grounder, he walked Babe Phelps, Cookie Lavagetto and Dolf Camilli to load the bases. But after a chat with manager Bill McKechnie, he settled down. Vander Meer got Ernie Koy to hit into a potential double-play grounder, but third baseman Lou Riggs elected to go for the force at home, preserving the shutout but leaving the no-hitter at risk. Dodgers player-manager Leo Durocher came to bat as the last man with a chance to spoil the no-hitter. On the second pitch, he popped up to center and Vander Meer joined the ranks of the immortals. The Dutch Master then tossed three more hitless innings in his next start against Boston before Debs Garms singled, halting his hitless string at 21 innings.

MOST HITS, ONE SEASON

262: Ichiro Suzuki, Seattle Mariners, 2004

It is sobering to think how many batting records Ichiro Suzuki might now possess if he had begun his career in the US instead of joining the majors at age 27, after playing nine seasons in Japan. In 2004, the Mariners' marvel set his sights on George Sisler's record of 257 hits in a season. Sisler set the mark in 1920 with the St. Louis Browns and after 84 years it had begun to look like it might never be broken. After all, no player since 1930 had ever topped 240 hits with the exception of Suzuki himself, who rapped out 242 in his rookie campaign. Ichiro tied Sisler's record with a leadoff single against the Texas Rangers on October 1, then, two innings later he hit a hard grounder up the middle for his record-breaking 258th hit. Fireworks exploded after Suzuki's historic hit, creating a haze over Seattle's Safeco Field, as his teammates mobbed him at first base. With the fans still cheering, Ichiro ran over to the first-base seats and shook hands with Sisler's 81-year-old daughter, Frances Sisler Drochelman, and other members of the Hall of Famer's family, who had been flown in by the Mariners for the three-game series. "I think that's the most emotional I've ever gotten in my life," the normally stoic Suzuki said later.

MOST TRIPLES, ONE SEASON

36: Owen "Chief" Wilson, Pittsburgh Pirates, 1912

Some baseball records simply defy logical explanation. Heading the list is Chief Wilson's mind-boggling feat of legging out 36 triples in a 152-game season in 1912. That is 10 more triples than any other player since 1900 has collected and 22 more than Wilson himself amassed in his second-best season. At six foot two and 185 pounds, the left-handed hitting Pirates slugger was powerfully built and, unlike most triples hitters, not particularly fast. However, he did benefit from the spacious dimensions of his home field. Forbes Field may have been the best park ever for triples, and the Pirates led the NL in the department 30 of the 62 seasons they played there. Predictably, Wilson amassed 24 of his record 36 triples at home in 1912, usually, according to newspaper accounts, by smoking the ball over an outfielder's head. But even so, a lot of great Pirates (Honus Wagner, Max Carey, Paul Waner, Fred Clarke) played at Forbes Field, some of them great triples hitters, and none approached Wilson's feat. Incredibly enough, after 118 games, Wilson had already recorded 33 three-baggers and was on pace to collect 43. But the Buccaneers outfielder slowed down in the latter part of the season, hitting only three in his last 34 games.

MOST MVP AWARDS, CAREER

7: Barry Bonds, 1986 to 2007

The seven MVP Awards that were bestowed upon Barry Bonds during his 22-year career put the outfielder in a class of his own. No other MLB player has ever won more than three, and only the NHL's Wayne Gretzky, with nine, has won more in any of the four major sports in North America. Bonds captured his first MVP in 1990 with the Pittsburgh Pirates, when he hit .301 with 33 home runs and 114 RBIs and stole 52 bases. He won again in 1992, hitting .311 with 34 homers and 103 RBIs and lifting the Pirates to their third-straight NL East Division title. In 1993, after signing a then-record six-year $43-million free-agent contract with San Francisco, he won his third MVP Award, batting .336 and leading the NL with 46 home runs and 123 RBIs. Bonds continued to produce throughout the 1990s, but was not in contention for the MVP again until 2000, when he finished second in voting to teammate Jeff Kent. Then followed an amazing run of four straight MVP Awards during a four-year span in which Bonds cracked 209 homers, including a record 73 in 2001, and posted off-the-chart slugging averages and on-base percentages. He won his last MVP at age 40, making him the oldest winner not just in baseball, but in any of North America's four major-league sports.

MOST CY YOUNG AWARDS, CAREER

7: Roger Clemens, 1984 to 2007

In addition to his record seven Cy Young Awards, Roger Clemens topped his league in ERA on seven occasions, led six times in shutouts, five times in strikeouts and four times in wins. Like Barry Bonds, Clemens's reputation has been sullied by accusations of steroid use, and like Bonds he also experienced a miraculous career revival after reaching his mid-30s. In Clemens's case, the rebound followed his exit from Boston in 1996, where Red Sox general manager Dan Duquette declared that Clemens was in the "twilight of his career" following four seasons in which he was a mediocre 40–39. Clemens signed with the Toronto Blue Jays and won the Cy Young Award in both of his two seasons with the Jays, as well as two pitching Triple Crowns (leading the AL in wins, strikeouts and ERA). After leaving Toronto, he went on to have several more spectacular years, going 20–3 with New York in 2001 and 18–4 with Houston in 2004, where he won his seventh Cy Young at a record age of 42. The Texan nearly won the honor an eighth time in 2005, when he logged a 1.87 ERA, the lowest in the majors, the lowest of his 22-season career and the lowest by a National Leaguer since Greg Maddux in 1995. However, Clemens posted a lackluster 13–8 record, primarily because the Astros provided him with such terrible run support, being shut out in nine of his 32 starts.

MOST CONSECUTIVE COMPLETE GAMES, CAREER

187: Jack Taylor, June 20, 1901 to August 9, 1906

Jack Taylor owns what may be the least known of all of baseball's "unbreakable" records. From midway through 1901 to the middle of the 1906 season, he completed every one of his starting assignments for the St. Louis Cardinals and the Chicago Cubs, a mind-boggling string of 187 games. (The last pitcher to throw even 20 complete games in a single season was the Dodgers' Fernando Valenzuela in 1986.) During his record-setting streak, Taylor won 20 or more games in three straight seasons and was the NL's ERA champion in 1902. In an era when a club's starters were expected to go the distance, none of Taylor's famous contemporaries came close to approaching his mark. Christy Mathewson, who completed 434 of his career 551 starts, never had a single season in which he completed every start. The great Walter Johnson, who led the AL in complete games six times, had only two years in which he finished every one of his starts. Yet Taylor managed the astonishing feat for four straight seasons, never starting less than 31 games in any of them. During his record streak, Taylor appeared in 202 games, starting and completing 187 of them (including an 18-inning and 19-inning game) and also pitched both ends of a doubleheader. He also made 15 relief appearances, finishing the game each time. His win-loss record over that span was 101–88.

MOST STRIKEOUTS BY A PITCHER, ONE SEASON

383: Nolan Ryan, California Angels, 1973

When Nolan Ryan took the mound for his final start of the 1973 season, he faced a daunting task: he needed 15 strikeouts to equal Sandy Koufax's single-season record of 382. California's opponent, the Minnesota Twins, nearly knocked Ryan out of the game in the early going, but after a couple of shaky innings "The Express" got rolling. When he fanned Steve Brye in the eighth inning, it gave Ryan 15 Ks and a share of the record. However, the Angels flamethrower, who was suffering from leg cramps, did not get a strikeout in the ninth. Fortunately for him, the game was tied 4–4 and went into extra innings. Ryan again failed to notch a strikeout in the 10th, but the game remained tied. Then, with one out in the 11th, Rod Carew drew a walk, Ryan's seventh of the game. The next batter, Tony Oliva, flied out to center and the Twins sent up pinch-hitter Rich Reese. Throwing pure heat, Ryan fanned Reese on three straight pitches to eclipse Koufax's record. Since the Angels scored in the bottom of the inning to win the game 5–4, Ryan set the mark with his last pitch of 1973. It's worth noting that this was the first year of the designated hitter. If AL pitchers had been batting that season, Ryan's strikeout total could have easily been up around 425.

MOST CONSECUTIVE SAVES, CAREER

84: Éric Gagné, Los Angeles Dodgers, August 26, 2002 to July 5, 2004

No one could have predicted Éric Gagné's amazing dominance as a reliever. The Montreal-born pitcher made his big-league debut with the Dodgers in 1999, two years after having Tommy John surgery to repair his elbow, and spent the next three years as a mediocre starter until the club converted him to a closer in 2002. Gagné blossomed in the bullpen. He reached 100 career saves in only his second season of relief, making him the fastest hurler ever to do so. Then, in 2003, he saved 55 consecutive games, which, when added to the eight consecutive saves he made at the end of 2002, gave him 63 in a row, a new big-league record. Gagné finished the year with a 1.20 ERA and an eye-popping 137 strikeouts in 82⅓ innings, earning himself the nickname "Game Over." He also claimed the Cy Young, becoming the only pitcher to win the award while having a losing season (his record was 2–3). In 2004, Gagné notched 21 more straight saves to push the record to 84 games, before finally blowing a two-run lead against Arizona on July 5. In the 23-month period in which Gagné was perfect, all the other relievers in the majors combined to blow 969 saves. During the streak, Gagné's ERA was 0.82, he fanned 14.3 hitters per nine innings and allowed only 4.1 hits per nine innings. Simply insane.

LOWEST EARNED-RUN AVERAGE, CAREER
(MINIMUM 1,000 INNINGS)

1.82: Ed Walsh, 1904 to 1917

Ed Walsh was clearly aided by playing during baseball's dead-ball era and in pitcher-friendly Comiskey Park. Still, there is no denying his dominance. Walsh threw what was probably the most effective spitball in history, a pitch that was legal at the time. His spitter had fantastic movement, but the White Sox hurler was still able to throw it with outstanding control, making it devastating to batters accustomed to seeing mostly fastballs and curves. As Detroit's Sam Crawford once remarked: "I think that ball disintegrated on the way to the plate, and the catcher put it back together again." Walsh joined the Pale Hose in 1904, and in 1906 he led the AL with 10 shutouts. His heroics continued into October, as he won two games, struck out 17 and allowed only one earned run in 15 innings in his team's World Series victory. The next year the Sox struggled to score in Walsh's starts, but he still posted a 24–18 record with a 1.60 ERA. Walsh had his greatest season in 1908, going 40–15 with a 1.42 ERA and leading the AL in complete games (42), shutouts (11), strikeouts (269) and innings (464) to become the last pitcher to throw more than 400 innings in a season. Walsh developed a tired arm in 1913 and never again approached his earlier highs. He ended his career with 195 wins, 126 losses and an absurdly low ERA of 1.82.

BEST STRIKEOUT-TO-HOME-RUN RATIO,
CAREER (MINIMUM 250 HOMERS)

1.02: Joe DiMaggio, 1936 to 1951

Joe DiMaggio's 361 home runs and only 369 strikeouts is an almost unknown statistic, yet it is startling in its comparative dimensions. Reggie Jackson struck out more than four times for each homer he hit. Mickey Mantle's ratio was three to one. Willie Mays fanned more than two times for every homer he hit. Even Ted Williams, often referred to as the best pure hitter ever, had 709 strikeouts for his 521 dingers. And what about the great contact hitters, the guys who choked up on the bat and didn't swing for the fences? Pete Rose fanned 1,143 times, while Rod Carew went down on strikes 1,028 times. But in 13 seasons, DiMaggio never fanned more than 39 times. In fact, until his last year, he was more likely to hit a homer than to strike out. How do we explain this? Well, even though DiMaggio hit the ball hard, his swing was fluid with an incredible follow-through. He had an exceptionally wide stance that gave him a controlled short stride, strong wrists that generated enormous power and the ability to wait until the last instant before lashing into a pitch. As phenomenal as DiMaggio's ratio is, it would have been even better had he not played half his games at Yankee Stadium, the toughest power park for right-handed hitters. At the time, left-center field, known as "Death Valley," extended 457 feet from home plate.

MOST RUNS BATTED IN, CAREER

2,297: Hank Aaron, 1954 to 1976

Although Hank Aaron's hallowed career home-run mark fell to Barry
Bonds in August 2007, his career RBI record remains intact, a full 301
clear of Bonds and 84 ahead of Babe Ruth, who ranks second. Ham-
merin' Hank surpassed Ruth's RBI total on May 1, 1975, while serving
as a designated hitter with the Milwaukee Brewers, more than a year
after he broke the Bambino's home-run record. Sustained excellence
over decades was the key to many of Aaron's records, including his RBI
standard. He topped 100 RBIs in 11 seasons and led the NL in the category four times, including a career high of 132 in 1957, the year he
sparked the Braves to a World Series triumph over the Yankees. Even so,
132 RBIs pales in comparison with Lou Gehrig, who drove in more than
150 runners in seven seasons, and Ruth who did it five times. But then
again, Aaron set few single-season records during his storied career. He
never, for example, hit more than 47 homers in a season, which is hard
to fathom, especially considering the number has been exceeded by
such clearly inferior players as Brady Anderson, Adrian Beltre and Greg
Vaughn. Yet Aaron still clouted 755 round-trippers before he retired, a
striking testament to his longevity and consistency.

MOST WORLD SERIES HOME RUNS, CAREER

18: Mickey Mantle, 1951 to 1968

By today's standards, Mickey Mantle was not a big guy—only five foot eleven and 198 pounds. But nobody swung as hard or hit the ball farther. As he once noted, "I hated striking out, but I always tried to kill the ball. I wanted to make it explode." In fact, it was a monstrous homer that Mantle belted out of Washington's Griffith Stadium on April 17, 1953 that gave rise to the term "tape-measure home run." Yankees PR director Red Patterson retrieved the ball and paced off the distance it had traveled, a reported 565 feet. The long-ball specialist was at his best in the bright spotlight of October. Three times he crushed three homers in a Series; in 1956 against Brooklyn, in 1960 against Pittsburgh and in 1964 against St. Louis. All told, Mantle registered a record 18 round trippers in the Fall Classic, three more than Babe Ruth. No active player has hit more than four. Mantle also tops the World Series leader board for most RBIs (40), runs (42) and total bases (123). None of these intimidating numbers is likely to be surpassed. Getting to the World Series is a difficult task, and making multiple appearances is even tougher. They don't build dynasties like the Yankees of Mantle's era. Amazingly, the Hall of Famer played in 12 Fall Classics in his first 14 seasons in the majors.

HIGHEST STRIKEOUT RATIO PER
NINE INNINGS BY A STARTER, ONE SEASON

13.4: Randy Johnson, Arizona Diamondbacks, 2001

Randy Johnson was hell on hitters. The scowling, six-foot-10 beanstalk threw with such ferocity that a filling once dislodged from his tightly clenched jaw and fell out of his mouth. His fastball regularly hit 98 mph and he had a nasty slider that sliced over the plate at around 90 mph. Johnson beat up on birds too. At a 2001 spring training game, one of his burners struck and vaporized a dove that was flying in front of home plate. At least it was a quick death; batters died all season long against him. In 2001, the Big Unit went 21–5 with a 2.49 ERA and 372 strikeouts. He fanned 13.4 batters for every nine innings he pitched, an all-time record. In fact, Johnson owns seven of the top 10 ratios in history. The 2001 performance came in the midst of one of the most dominating four-year pitching runs in baseball annals. From 1999 to 2002, Johnson went 81–27 with a 2.39 ERA and 1,417 strikeouts, comparable to Sandy Koufax's reign of terror from 1963 to 1966 with the Dodgers, when he went 97–27 with a 1.86 ERA and 1,228 strikeouts, especially if we factor in adjusted ERA, which makes Johnson's ERA 77 percent better than that of the average pitcher of the time, compared to Koufax at 72 percent. Johnson also won the Cy Young in each of those four seasons.

47

MOST GAMES MANAGED, CAREER

7,755: Connie Mack, 1894 to 1950

Connie Mack managed more major-league games than the total games played by 12 of baseball's current franchises, and nearly 3,000 more games than runner-up John McGraw. He also holds the managerial records for wins (3,731) and losses (3,948), with his victory total being almost 1,000 more than any other manager. Mack piloted the Philadephia Athletics for the club's first 50 years before retiring at age 87 after the 1950 season, and was also the team's part-owner from 1901 to 1954. He was the first manager to win the World Series three times, and is the only manager to win consecutive Series on separate occasions (1910/1911 and 1929/1930); his five World Series titles remain the third most by any manager, and his nine AL pennants rank second in league history. However, Mack, who had no income outside of baseball and was forced to sell off his talent and rebuild during challenging financial times, also saw his teams finish in last place 17 times. From 1934 to 1950, his A's enjoyed only three winning seasons. A quiet, even-tempered and gentlemanly man, who always wore a suit instead of a baseball uniform, Mack was one of the first managers to work on repositioning his fielders during the game, often directing the outfielders by waving his scorecard from the bench.

MOST CONSECUTIVE WINS BY A PITCHER, CAREER

24: Carl Hubbell, New York Giants, July 17, 1936 to May 27, 1937

Known affectionately as "The Meal Ticket" by fans of the New York Giants during the Depression years, Hubbell was the NL's premier left-handed pitcher of the 1930s and one of the finest in modern baseball history. He won 21 or more games each year from 1933 to 1937 and led his team to the World Series in 1933, 1936 and 1937. Hubbell became a household name at the 1934 All-Star Game, when he used his wicked screwball to strike out Babe Ruth, Lou Gehrig, Jimmie Foxx, Al Simmons and Joe Cronin in succession. But Hubbell's greatest feat occurred two years later when the Missouri-born southpaw won 24 consecutive games without a loss. The first 18 victories came in 1936 as he sparked the Giants to the pennant, and the second six were recorded in 1937. The streak began in July 1936, with a 6–0 shutout win over the Pirates, and ended on May 31, 1937, when the Dodgers defeated Hubbell and the Giants 10–3 in the first game of a doubleheader before 61,756 fans at the Polo Grounds. The Dodgers drove Hubbell from the hill after 3 ⅓ innings, stinging him for seven hits and five earned runs. During the streak, the Giants' mainstay won 22 games as a starter and two in relief, and also pitched 19 complete games.

MOST TOTAL BASES, ONE GAME

19: Shawn Green, Los Angeles Dodgers, May 23, 2002

No player has broken out of a slump in a more spectacular fashion than Shawn Green, who entered this 2002 game against Milwaukee hitting a paltry .238 with three homers. The assault began modestly: in his first at-bat, Green drove in a run with a double off pitcher Glendon Rusch. The next time up, he hit a three-run blast off Rusch; then he stung reliever Brian Mallette for solo homers in the fourth and fifth. By then, Los Angeles was up 10–1 and cruising. But there were still four innings to play and at least two chances for the suddenly torrid Dodger outfielder to hit a record-tying fourth home run. Jose Cabrera was pitching when Green led off the eighth and got his puniest hit of the day, a single to center. Fortunately for Green, the Dodgers scored four times in the ninth, giving him another shot at history. With two outs he delivered, jolting a Cabrera pitch 450 feet over the right-center-field fence. It was the perfect exclamation point to a spectacular day. Not only did Green become just the 14th player to hit four dingers in one game, he also set a record with his 19 total bases, eclipsing Joe Adcock's mark of 18, set with the 1954 Milwaukee Braves. Throw in six hits in six at-bats, six runs and seven RBIs, and you have a supernatural performance.

MOST SEASONS HITTING 60 HOME RUNS

3: Sammy Sosa, Chicago Cubs, 1998, 1999, 2001

It was not too long ago that a 60-homer season was regarded as the Mt. Everest of baseball achievements. Babe Ruth's iconic record of 60 homers lasted 34 years until Roger Maris broke it by hitting 61 in 1961. Maris's mark endured 37 years until Mark McGwire and Sammy Sosa both vaporized it in 1998, as McGwire clubbed 70 and Sosa blasted 66. McGwire would lead the majors again in 1999 with 65 homers, two more than Sosa, but the muscular first-sacker then tailed off badly. Sosa, however, continued to pile up titanic long-ball numbers, slamming 50 out of the park in 2000, and 64 in 2001. This gave the Cubs outfielder a total of 233 homers for the four seasons from 1998 to 2002, an astounding average of 61 per year. Over that span he also averaged 149 RBIs per year. This represents one of the most impressive stretches of power-hitting in baseball history, but oddly, it's a feat that has slipped most people's notice. The reason may be connected to Sosa's rumored steroid use, because he was caught using a corked bat in 2003, or simply because the Dominican lost his much-hyped 1998 homer showdown with McGwire, and never set a single-season MLB record. Whatever the cause, there is no ignoring those three seasons of 60-plus homers.

LOWEST EARNED-RUN AVERAGE, ONE SEASON

0.96: Dutch Leonard, Boston Red Sox, 1914

It is hard to know what to make of Dutch Leonard, a talented, but widely disliked dead-ball era pitcher who is most famous for sparking one of the biggest scandals in baseball history. When he retired in 1925, Leonard accused Ty Cobb and Tris Speaker of conspiring to throw a 1919 baseball game, when the hurler was a teammate of Cobb on the Detroit Tigers, a move that nearly led to their lifetime banishment. Before that however, Leonard won three World Series with the Boston Red Sox, and in 1914 he went 19–5 while registering a microscopic 0.96 ERA in 224 ⅔ innings. Because the 22-year-old's season was curtailed by an injury in September, the lefty failed to win 20 games and, except for ERA (a new stat in the AL), did not lead the league in any major pitching category. As a result, his performance went largely unheralded in the press, as is clear by his 16th-place finish in the AL MVP voting. Even Leonard regarded his work that year as incomplete. As he later admitted in an interview, "If I hadn't broken my wrist I think I would have done very well that year." Whatever magic he channeled in 1914, Leonard never again came close to duplicating his dazzling sophomore stats, eventually concluding his 11-year career with a 139–113 record, 13 shutouts and a 2.76 ERA.

MOST CONSECUTIVE GAMES WITH A RUN BATTED IN

17: Ray Grimes, Chicago Cubs, June 27 to July 23, 1922

This impressive record has never received much attention, partly because it was not discovered until fairly recently, but also because it was set by an obscure player. If the record belonged to Ty Cobb or Babe Ruth, it would have a much higher profile. Ray Grimes, the player who set the record, made the majors in 1920 and lasted for six seasons in the bigs. He became the Chicago Cubs starting first-sacker in 1921, and had an excellent rookie year, batting .321. In 1922, he hit .354, second in the NL to Rogers Hornsby, and drove in 99 runs, 26 of which came during his record-setting 17-game streak. The streak began in the second game of a doubleheader with Pittsburgh on June 27. The next day Grimes had lumbago and sat out. He was back in the lineup on June 30 and had at least one RBI per game until a July 8 twinbill. He played only one inning of the second game, but notched an RBI single before leaving the game with a wrenched back. The injury was serious, and he did not return to action until July 18 when he celebrated with a homer, double and two singles in a 6–3 win over the Phils. The streak continued until July 25, when Grimes failed to drive in any runs against Boston. His big chance came in the fourth inning with two Cubbies on base, but he was walked to load the bases. During the streak, Grimes batted a sizzling .432.

MOST HOME RUNS BY A SWITCH-HITTER, CAREER

536: Mickey Mantle, 1951 to 1968

The switch-hitting power hitter remains a rare species, but the breed was even rarer when Mickey Mantle burst onto the big-league scene in the early 1950s. Mantle was taught to switch-hit as a child by his father, Elvin "Mutt" Mantle, an Oklahoma lead miner and avid baseball fan, who named his first son after Hall of Fame catcher Mickey Cochrane. Young Mickey would use his natural right-handed swing against his left-handed father, then turn around and bat left-handed against his right-handed grandfather. The tutelage paid off; Mantle eventually became baseball's most feared switch-hitter, slamming 536 career homers and 1,509 RBIs. He also owns the record for the highest single-season batting average (.365) for a switch-hitter, a mark he set in 1957, as well as for single-season homers (54), set in 1961. And too, in 1956, the Mick became the only switch-hitter to win a Triple Crown, leading both the AL and the majors with 52 homers, 130 RBIs and a .353 batting average. Although the Yankee icon considered himself a better right-handed hitter, he actually poled more homers from the portside: 372 left-handed to 164 right-handed. This was largely due to Mantle batting left-handed much more often, as the majority of pitchers are right-handed, but also because the outfield fences in his home park, Yankee Stadium, were much closer in right.

MOST STRIKEOUTS BY A PITCHER IN NINE INNINGS

20: Roger Clemens, Boston Red Sox, April 29, 1986
20: Roger Clemens, Boston Red Sox, September 18, 1996
20: Kerry Wood, Chicago Cubs, May 6, 1998
20: Randy Johnson, Arizona Diamondbacks, May 8, 2001

When you strike out 20 batters in a game you have to be throwing some serious gas. All three of these pitchers had high-octane stuff. Was one performance better than the others? The nod goes to Kerry Wood. Roger Clemens, who twice racked up 20 punch-outs, did it first against Seattle, allowing three hits in a 3–1 win. The second time, he tossed a 4–0, four-hit shutout against Detroit. Randy Johnson posted 20 Ks against the Cincinnati Reds, but left after the ninth inning with the score tied 1–1. Wood managed the feat in only his fifth major-league start. At age 20, he was the second-youngest player in the majors at the time. The Cubs rookie bamboozled Houston, the Central Division's top team, with a blur of fastballs and diving curves and sliders in his masterpiece, allowing one hit on an infield single, hitting one batter and walking no one. Watching from Houston's dugout that day was C.J. Nitkowski, who was also on the Tigers, the team that Clemens stifled in 1996, and also played for the Braves in 2004 when Randy Johnson pitched a perfecto against Atlanta. "Neither compared to what Kerry did that day," Nitkowski said.

MOST YEARS LEADING THE LEAGUE IN WINS, CAREER

8: Warren Spahn, 1942 to 1965

Warren Spahn was a cagey pitcher who loved the psychological battle with batters. He once summed up his approach on the mound by declaring: "Hitting is timing. Pitching is upsetting timing." But Spahn was also mentally and physically tough—during World War II he fought in the Battle of the Bulge and won a Bronze Star and a Purple Heart. Spahn won 363 games in his 21-year career, the most by any southpaw in history. He won 20 games 13 times and led the NL in wins a record eight times, two more titles than Bob Feller and Walter Johnson chalked up in the AL. At age 42, he copped his last title, posting a 23–7 record in 1963. On July 2 of that season, the Milwaukee Braves lefty hooked up with 25-year-old San Francisco Giants ace Juan Marichal in a titanic pitching duel. The two hurlers both tossed scoreless ball until Willie Mays won the game for the Giants with a home run in the bottom of the 16th. Marichal threw 227 pitches in his complete game 1–0 win, while Spahn threw 201 in the loss, allowing nine hits and one walk. Hall of Famer Carl Hubbell, who was in attendance that night, said of Spahn, "He ought to will his body to medical science." Incredibly, in the game before this epic, Spahn pitched a complete-game shutout, beating the Dodgers 1–0. In the game following it, he blanked Houston 4–0 on a complete-game five-hitter.

56

MOST CONSECUTIVE BATTERS
RETIRED BY A PITCHER, ONE SEASON

45: Mark Buehrle, Chicago White Sox, July 2009

All perfect games are unlikely, but Mark Buehrle's perfecto against the Tampa Bay Rays on July 23, 2009, was a real stunner. The White Sox lefty was facing a batting order with four All-Stars, in a ballpark (U.S. Cellular Field) that was surrendering more home runs per game than Coors Field, Colorado's famous launching pad. Moreover, Buehrle's battery mate, Ramon Castro, was catching Buehrle for the first time. But the scruffy-looking southpaw came out throwing strikes, setting the Rays down in order on 10 pitches in the first, and rode his early momentum, mowing down Tampa Bay's hitters with rapid-fire precision. He had only one close call. Gabe Kapler, the leadoff hitter in the ninth, smashed a long fly to left-center field that outfielder DeWayne Wise snared with a dramatic juggling act at the wall. After 116 pitches the Rays were done, 27 up, 27 down. Final score: 5–0. In his next start against the Minnesota Twins, Buehrle picked up where he had left off, retiring the first 17 Twins batters to surpass the record of 41 straight set by San Francisco's Jim Barr in 1972 and tied by Buehrle's teammate Bobby Jenks, a reliever, in 2007. Buehrle's bid for a second consecutive perfect game ended with a walk to Alexi Casilla with two outs in the sixth. Then Denard Span followed with a single to break up the no-hitter.

MOST WINS BY A ROOKIE PITCHER, ONE SEASON

28: Grover Cleveland Alexander, Philadelphia Phillies, 1911

Grover Alexander's nickname was "Old Pete," which seems fitting as it is impossible to find a photo of him in which he looks young, even as a rookie. Alexander was certainly not a stylish player: he was ungainly, with a shambling walk; his uniform never seemed to fit properly, and his cap looked a size too small and stood on his head at a precarious tilt. Yet his pitching motion was economical, apparently effortless and graceful. He came at the batter with an easy sidearm motion and excellent control of his fastball and curve. "He looked like he was hardly working at all, like he was throwing batting practice," said one teammate. The Phillies acquired Alexander from Syracuse of the New York State League for $750. It proved quite a bargain. In his 1911 debut, the 24-year-old led the NL with 28 wins, 31 complete games, 367 innings pitched and seven shutouts. His 227 strikeouts, good for second in the league, stood as the record for rookies until Herb Score gunned down 245 batters for the Indians in 1955. Several rookie pitchers in the dead-ball era posted win totals that would be unthinkable in today's game, including Russ Ford with 26 for the Yankees in 1910 and Larry Cheney with 26 for the Cubs in 1912, but none went on to enjoy as much success as Alexander, who retired with 373 victories, third all-time behind only Cy Young and Walter Johnson.

58

MOST STEALS OF HOME, CAREER

54: Ty Cobb, 1905 to 1928

There are several requirements needed for stealing home: speed, daring, quick reflexes and an ability to read pitchers. Ty Cobb possessed all four, plus a fifth trait—naked aggression. He was not averse to leaping into a catcher with his spikes raised in order to jar the ball loose. Cobb pilfered home 54 times, which is 21 times more than Max Carey did, who ranks second. Cobb also holds the single-season record for steals of home with eight, set in 1912. His boldness on the base paths is aptly illustrated by a game against Philadelphia on July 12, 1911. In the first inning, he drew a walk off lefty Harry Krause, then, on consecutive pitches, he swiped second, third and home. All told, Cobb "stole for the cycle" a record four times during his career. The Georgia Peach also stole home four times with the Athletics in 1927, when he was over 40. Of these four games, his biggest day was April 26, 1927. In a 9–8 win over Boston, he cracked three hits, including a double that drove in the winning run; he also walked and stole home in the seventh inning as the relief pitcher was about to deliver his first pitch. Then, in the ninth, Cobb made a shoestring catch in shallow right and trapped the runner off first for an unassisted double play that ended the game.

MOST DOUBLE PLAYS BY AN OUTFIELDER, CAREER

139: Tris Speaker, 1907 to 1928

Tris Speaker hit for average, lashed extra-base hits, stole bases and played one of the best center fields in history. He was famous for playing extraordinarily shallow, and his great speed and uncanny ability to read the ball off the bat allowed him to be in Babe Ruth's words, a "fifth infielder." Ruth swore he saw Speaker throw out a man at first base from center field on several occasions. This ability to cover his position is even more remarkable in a day when the fences were often 450 feet or more from home plate. Twice in 1914, with the Boston Red Sox, Speaker executed an unassisted double play at second base, snaring low line drives on the run and then beating base runners to the bag. He repeated this feat in 1918 with the Cleveland Indians, and turned a record six of them during his career. At least once he was credited as the pivot man in a routine double play. Catcher Bill Carrigan, a long-time teammate of Speaker's on the Red Sox, would often send a pickoff throw from his position to Speaker, who had sneaked in to second base. Speaker is still the all-time leader in outfield assists (448) and double plays (139). In comparison, Willie Mays, who many consider the best center fielder of all time, only recorded 195 total assists and 51 double plays, despite playing 203 more games than Speaker.

60

MOST CONSECUTIVE SEASONS WITH 100 RUNS BATTED IN

13: Lou Gehrig, 1926 to 1938

13: Jimmie Foxx, 1929 to 1941

Lou Gehrig and Jimmy Foxx were two of the most feared sluggers in baseball annals. Batting cleanup in the Yankees' power-laden lineup, Gehrig drove in 1,990 runs during his career, and had seven seasons in which he amassed 150 RBIs or more, topped by an AL record 184 in 1931. Along the way the Iron Horse also played in a record 2,130 straight games, hauled the Yankees to seven pennants and became, in his quiet way, perhaps the greatest first baseman of all time. Gehrig's main rival for the title was Foxx, a brawny Maryland farm boy who would cut off his shirt sleeves to display his bulging biceps. "Even his hair has muscles," an opposing pitcher complained. Baseballs flew off Foxx's bat like heat-seeking missiles. He once hit a ball with such force that it smashed a seat in the upper corner of the third deck of Yankee Stadium. Like Gehrig, Foxx was an RBI machine. He topped 150 RBIs in five seasons, reaching a career high of 175 in 1938 with the Boston Red Sox. The duo's shared record of 13 consecutive 100 RBI seasons was not seriously challenged for more than seven decades, but Alex Rodriguez, who compiled his twelfth- straight 100-RBI season in 2009, now has a chance to equal or break it.

HIGHEST WINNING PERCENTAGE BY A PITCHER, CAREER

.690: Whitey Ford, 1950 to 1967

All Whitey Ford did was win. As a rookie in 1950, he won his first eight starts. During his first 14 seasons, the little left-hander only twice posted a record that was as low as three games over .500, and in 12 seasons he was at least six games over .500. Unlike many Hall of Fame hurlers, Ford was not a power pitcher. Instead, he relied on a mix of pitches (including the occasional illegal one), intelligence and guile to foil hitters. Although he was fortunate to play for a Yankee powerhouse, Ford's stats would likely have been even better if not for manager Casey Stengel's insistence on limiting his "banty rooster" to 250 innings a season, and using him mostly against first-division teams. After Stengel was replaced by Ralph Houk in 1961, Ford was given more work and that year he went 25–4 with a league-high 39 starts and 283 innings pitched, winning the Cy Young Award. Two years later, he rang up a 24–7 record, and again led the AL with 37 starts and 269 innings pitched. During his 18-year career, Ford won 236 games and lost 106, giving him a .690 winning percentage, the highest in history by a pitcher with a minimum of 300 decisions. Famed for his poise in big-game situations, Ford also holds the record for most World Series wins (10) and strikeouts (94).

MOST WINS BY A PITCHER, ONE SEASON

41: Jack Chesbro, New York Highlanders, 1904

Jack Chesbro was known as "Happy Jack," but "Slippery Jack" would have been more apt. Chesbro was the majors' first spitball artist. He mastered the then-legal pitch with the Pittsburgh Pirates in 1902 and became a star, topping the NL with a 28–6 record and a 2.17 ERA. In 2003, Chesbro jumbed to the AL's newly formed New York Highlanders (who became the Yankees in 1913) and pitched the franchise's first game. He won 21 games for New York in 2003, but in 2004 he turned in a season for the ages. The rubber-armed Chesbro appeared in 55 games, starting 51 and finishing 49, pitched 454 ⅔ innings and posted a record of 41–12 along with a 1.82 ERA. Unfortunately, the glow of his magical season was erased by the last pitch he threw. On the final day of the season, Chesbro started the opening game of a doubleheader against the first-place Boston Pilgrims with the Highlanders needing to sweep both games to cop the pennant. In the top of the ninth, with the score tied 2–2 and Boston's Lou Criger on the third base, Chesbro uncorked a spitter that sailed past catcher Red Kleinow, and Criger raced home with what turned out to be the pennant-clinching run. The stigma attached to that loss haunted the hurler for the rest of his life, and for years afterwards Chesbro's wife campaigned unsuccessfully to have the scorer's call changed from a wild pitch to a passed ball.

HIGHEST WINNING PERCENTAGE BY
A 20-GAME WINNER, ONE SEASON

.893: Ron Guidry, New York Yankees, 1978

Some time during the 1978 season they began calling Ron Guidry "Louisiana Lightning." It may have started after he fanned a Yankee-record 18 batters on June 17 in a game against the California Angels that launched the Yankee Stadium tradition of fans standing and clapping for a strikeout with two strikes on the opposing batter. Whenever it started it was an apt moniker, as few pitchers have had a more electrifying season. The Cajun southpaw went 25–3, led the loop with a sparkling 1.74 ERA (the lowest by an AL lefty since Dutch Leonard's 0.96 in 1914), nine shutouts, 248 strikeouts and 6.15 hits allowed per nine innings pitched. He held batters to a .193 batting average, .249 on base percentage and .279 slugging percentage. New York's record in Guidry's 35 starts was 30–5. His sensational pitching was the main reason that the Yankees were able to overtake the Boston Red Sox after trailing in the AL East by 14 games on July 18. Guidry capped the comeback by nailing down his 25th win in the Yankees' 5–4 triumph over the Red Sox in a one-game playoff to decide the division winner. Oddly, all three of Guidry's losses in 1978 were to left-handed pitchers named Mike: Mike Flanagan of the Orioles, Mike Caldwell of the Brewers and Mike Willis of the Blue Jays.

MOST GOLD GLOVES BY A POSITION PLAYER, CAREER

16: Brooks Robinson, 1955 to 1977

When he hung up his cleats in 1977 after a 23-year career with the Baltimore Orioles, Brooks Robinson held every lifetime fielding mark (assists, putouts, double plays and fielding average) for third base. The Human Vacuum Cleaner's dazzling credentials also included 16 consecutive Gold Glove Awards, the most ever won by a position player (pitcher Greg Maddux won 18). As umpire Ed Runge noted, "That kid plays third base like he came down from a higher league." Although his brilliance in the field often overshadowed his offensive abilities, Robinson was no slouch with the lumber. In 1964, he posted a .317 batting average with 28 homers and a league-leading 118 RBIs to win the AL MVP Award. Robinson made his biggest impression in the 1970 World Series, when he led Baltimore to a five-game triumph over the Cincinnati Reds. Besides making several sensational acrobatic stops at third, Robinson also batted .429 with nine hits and two homers and set a new World Series total-bases record with 17, to win the Series MVP. After watching the ceremony in which Robinson received a new Toyota as part of his award, Cincinnati catcher Johnny Bench quipped, "Gee! If we had known he wanted a new car that bad, we'd have chipped in and bought him one."

MOST STRIKEOUTS BY A ROOKIE PITCHER, ONE SEASON

276: Dwight Gooden, New York Mets, 1984

Dwight Gooden joined the New York Mets in 1984 straight out of Class-A Carolina League where he recorded 300 strikeouts in 191 innings. It was a big leap, but Davey Johnson, the Mets manager, was convinced he had the stuff to make the big club. Johnson was right. Armed with a high-riding fastball and a snapping curve, Gooden posted a 17–9 record, a 2.60 ERA and 276 strikeouts in only 218 innings—the most strikeouts in the majors in 1984 and an all-time record for rookies. The strikeouts earned him the nickname "Doctor K" (later shortened to "Doc") and a rooting section at New York's Shea Stadium that hung out a red "K" for each strikeout during his starts. He tied the major-league mark for strikeouts in two consecutive games, with 32 in starts on September 12 and 17, which, combined with his September 7 start, gave him a record 43 in three straight games. Equally amazing was the 19-year-old's average of 11.4 strikeouts per nine innings. Not even such fabled flamethrowers as Bob Feller, Sandy Koufax or Nolan Ryan had averaged 11 punch-outs per game for a season. In 1987, Ryan surpassed Gooden's mark, recording 270 strikeouts in 211 innings, a rate of 11.5 per game, but for one glittering season, a bone-lean black teenager from Florida was baseball's king of Ks.

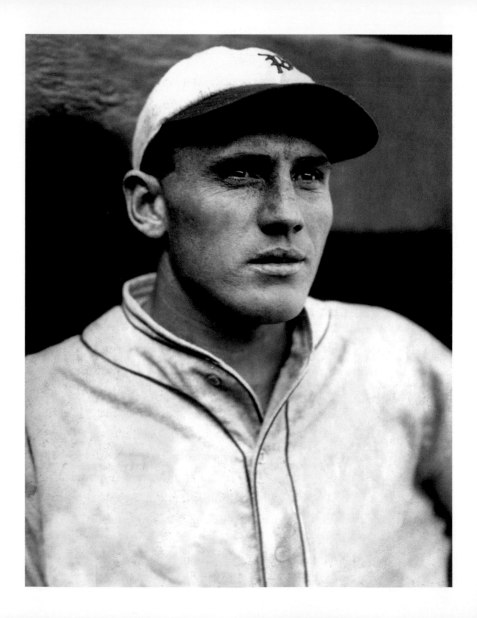

MOST ASSISTS BY AN OUTFIELDER, ONE SEASON

44: Chuck Klein, Philadelphia Phillies, 1930

In 1930, Chuck Klein enjoyed a monster season, ripping 250 hits, 59 doubles, 40 homers, 170 RBIs and a .386 batting average. That year, Klein also set a record for outfielders by amassing a staggering 44 assists, and led all NL ball hawks with 10 double plays. Although Klein had a strong throwing arm, he owes his assists' record to playing right field at Philadelphia's compact Baker Bowl, which was 281 feet to right field and 300 to right center. The right-field line was a mere 270 feet from home plate, and the wall itself was 40 feet high with a 20-foot-high screen on top. Because of the park's dollhouse dimensions, Klein played much closer to the infield than any modern outfielder. If Klein took up a position just 40 feet in front of the wall, he may have had a shorter throw to first base than the third baseman, which enabled him to throw out some batters at first base. He also became adept at fielding caroms off the corrugated tin wall. After being traded to the Cubs in 1934, Klein's offensive and defensive numbers declined, partly due to leaving Baker Bowl, but also because of injuries and a growing problem with alcohol. Even so, he still managed to throw out 20 runners in 2,145 innings a respectable rate of 9.32 per 1,000 innings, but far below his rate of 15.02 per 1,000 innings in Philadelphia.

MOST SHUTOUTS BY A PITCHER, ONE SEASON

16: Grover Cleveland Alexander, Philadelphia Phillies, 1916

Grover Alexander overcame several physical ailments to become one of baseball's greatest pitchers. The litany of woe included being hit in the head by a ball in 1909 that knocked him unconscious for 56 hours and resulted in a case of double vision; a year spent as an artillery sergeant on the front in World War I that left him with shell shock and partial deafness; epileptic seizures that began to afflict him in 1919, and a long-running addiction to alcohol. In 1915, at age 28, Alexander turned in the first of three stunning seasons for Philadelphia, going 31–10 with a 1.22 ERA and 12 shutouts to lead the club to its first pennant and its first trip to the World Series. In 1916, the lanky right-hander went 33–12 with a 1.55 ERA and a major-league record 16 goose eggs. In 1917, he went 30–13 with a 1.83 ERA and eight shutouts. That's 94 wins over three seasons and 36 shutouts. The numbers are doubly impressive as he pitched his home games at Baker Bowl, which had the smallest dimensions of any major-league park. As a reward for his efforts, the financially strapped Phils traded Alexander to the Cubs, where he led the NL in wins, ERA and strikeouts in 1921. Despite worsening epileptic seizures and heavier drinking, Alexander pitched until 1930, recording 373 wins and 90 shutouts.

MOST HOME RUNS BY TWO TEAMMATES, ONE SEASON

115: Roger Maris (61) and Mickey Mantle (54), New York Yankees, 1961

In the summer of 1961, Roger Maris and Mickey Mantle waged an assault on Babe Ruth's single-season record of 60 home runs. Like Ruth, Mantle was an accomplished slugger, having already belted 321 homers over his 10-season career, and had a larger-than-life persona. But while Mantle was loved by baseball fans across America, Maris was quiet, unassuming and often surly with the press. Many did not feel he was worthy of challenging Ruth's record. On September 1, Maris had 51 home runs and Mantle had 48. Mantle lost his shot at the record when he suffered an infection and missed part of September, but Maris went on to hit 61, breaking Ruth's mark in the last game of the season. Mantle ended the year with 54 home runs. The pair's total of 115 homers cracked the two-man record of 107 that Ruth and Lou Gehrig had set in 1927. But the year held few fond memories for Maris, who lost clumps of hair due to the media pressure and the death threats he received. Speaking in 1980 he said: "They acted as though I was doing something wrong, poisoning the record books or something. Do you know what I have to show for 61 home runs? Nothing. Exactly nothing." What should have been one of baseball's greatest achievements became one of its saddest stories.

MOST POSTSEASON HOME RUNS, CAREER

29: Manny Ramirez, 1993 to 2009

On October 13, 2007, in the fifth inning of Game 2 of the American League Championship Series, Boston's Manny Ramirez belted his 23rd postseason homer off Cleveland Indians reliever Rafael Perez, passing the Yankees' Bernie Williams for the most of all-time. Ramirez has since added to his record total: as of 2009, it was up to 29, which, puts him comfortably ahead of the next closest active player: Derek Jeter, at 20. Although Man-Ram has a reputation for being a flake, it is worth noting that teams that had previously struggled in the postseason suddenly found ways to win after acquiring the dreadlocked slugger. When Ramirez joined the Cleveland Indians in 1993, the club had not made a postseason appearance since 1954 and had not won a postseason game since 1948. With Ramirez in tow, the Tribe had a 27–25 postseason record and made two World Series appearances. When he went to Boston in 2001, he joined a team that had a woeful five wins and 14 losses in 14 previous postseasons and had not captured a World Series since 1914. With Ramirez, the Red Sox went 28–15 in the postseason and won two World Series. When the Sox won their first in 2004, Ramirez batted .412 and was voted the Series MVP. Most recently, after being traded to Los Angeles during the 2008 campaign, Ramirez helped the Dodgers win their first postseason series since 1988.

70

MOST SAVES, ONE SEASON

62: Francisco Rodriguez, Los Angeles Angels, 2008

The saves record has grown through the years in steady increments. In 1961, Luis Arroyo held the record with 29. By 1966, it belonged to Jack Aker with 32. In 1972, John Hiller nudged the mark up to 38, and in 1986, Dave Righetti took it to 46. Then, in 1990, Bobby Thigpen extended it into completely new territory, notching 56 saves for the White Sox. There it stayed until 2008 when Francisco Rodriguez began piling up saves at a frantic pace. Using a fastball that consistently reached 91–94 mph, and a hard-biting curve, K-Rod set a major-league record by posting his 35th save before the All-Star break, breaking the mark of 34 set by the Braves' John Smoltz in 2003. The 26-year-old Venezuelan then went on to erase Thigpen's mark in a 5–2 win over Seattle on September 11, before finishing with 62 saves for the season. "He's fearless," said Angels manager Mike Scioscia. "I've been around a lot of good closers, but Frankie turns the page better than anyone I've seen." Unfortunately for the Angels, Rodriguez turned the page in a different direction at the end of the season, when he filed for free agency and signed a three-year $37-million deal with the New York Mets. The Mets can only hope that Rodriguez doesn't suffer the same fate as Thigpen. Only 27 years old when he set his record, he developed back problems and saved only 30 games in the rest of his career.

AGE OF OLDEST BATTING CHAMPION

40 years, 71 days: Barry Bonds, San Francisco Giants, 2004

Like Wayne Gretzky in hockey and Wilt Chamberlain in basketball, Barry Bonds owns a big chunk of real estate in his sport's record book. Unlike Gretzky and Chamberlain, however, Bonds set all of his records in the late stages of his career, thanks in large part, claim the critics, to a chemical assist from the Bay Area Laboratory Co-operative. Of all Bonds's records, the one that has attracted the least attention is his 2004 batting title. Bonds, who turned 40 on July 24 of that year, hit .362, the second-highest average of his career next to the .370 that he hit in 2002, at age 38. Before he turned 30, the best average that Bonds managed was .336 at age 29. By winning the 2004 title, Bonds surpassed former record-holder Ted Williams, who won his last batting title at 40 years and 29 days with a .328 average in 1958. Amazingly, Williams hit .388 the year before, capturing the 1957 batting crown at age 39. No one that old has ever hit anything close to that number, and no one has ever accused Williams of taking steroids. Despite being walked an astounding 232 times, Bonds also hit 45 homers in 2004, obliterating the record for 40-year-olds, set by Detroit's Darrell Evans, who clouted 34 in 1987. Of course, Evans played in Tiger Stadium, one of baseball's best hitting parks, while Bonds played at AT&T Park, one of the worst.

AGE OF YOUNGEST BATTING CHAMPION

20 years, 280 days, Al Kaline, Detroit Tigers, 1955

Just two years out of high school, 20-year-old Al Kaline, standing six feet two and weighing a raw-boned 157 pounds, batted .340 and won the AL batting title. The Tigers right fielder also topped the AL in hits and total bases. In doing so, the second-year pro became the youngest major leaguer to win a batting title. Although he finished second in MVP voting to Yogi Berra, based on their stats, Kaline should have won the award. Berra batted .272 with 84 runs, 147 hits, 27 homers and 108 RBIS, while Kaline batted .340 with 121 runs, 200 hits, 27 homers and 102 RBIS. The Tigers phenom would later come to regard his 1955 performance as a curse because fans expected greatness of him every year. As he said in a 1964 interview in *Sports Illustrated*: "Everybody said this guy's another Ty Cobb, another Joe DiMaggio. How much pressure can you take? What they didn't know is I'm not that good a hitter. I have to work as hard if not harder than anybody in the league." Kaline never posted a batting average that high again, though he did hit over .300 nine times in his career. A recipient of 10 Gold Gloves, Kaline possessed a strong arm and great instincts and once went 242 consecutive games without making an error. He retired with 3,007 hits, 399 homers, 1,583 RBIS and a .297 batting average.

MOST ALL-STAR GAME STARTS, CAREER

18: Willie Mays, 1954 to 1973

Ted Williams once declared, "They invented the All-Star Game for Willie Mays." Willams was right on the money. It was in the All-Star setting that the Giants center fielder thrived. "I loved to play in the All-Star Game," Mays recalled in the 1990s. "It was a fun thing for us. We didn't get bonuses like these kids do; I really didn't play for the money, anyway. I wanted to play to win, and I was a guy who played nine innings. I didn't want the American League beating me." Mays played in 24 All-Star Games and started in a record 18 of them. He set records for at-bats, hits, runs, extra-base hits, triples and stolen bases at the midsummer classic and was often his team's catalyst. Typical was the 1968 game at Houston's Astrodome, when at age 37, he earned his second All-Star Game MVP Award. In a season when pitchers dominated, Mays built the only run of the game when he led off the first inning with a single, took second on an error, went to third on a wild pitch and scored on a double-play grounder. Five years earlier, at Cleveland's Municipal Stadium in 1963, Mays had put on a one-man show to claim his first. Although he had only one hit, he drove in two runs and scored two. He also stole two bases and made the defensive play of the game, a running catch that deprived Joe Pepitone of extra bases in the eighth as the NL won 5–3.

MOST DOUBLES, CAREER

792: Tris Speaker, 1907 to 1928

Widely recognized as the greatest defensive outfielder of his era, Tris Speaker still holds the majors' career records for most assists (448) and double plays (139) by an outfielder. Sportswriter Grantland Rice likened Speaker's movements in the outfield to the "smoothness of a summer wind." The phrase "where triples go to die" was originally penned of Speaker's glove, but history somehow misplaced the attribution to Shoeless Joe Jackson. The Texan was also a superb hitter, with a career .344 batting average, 3,515 hits and an MLB record 792 doubles. To surpass Speaker's total of 792 two-baggers, a player would have to average 40 or more doubles for 20 years. Despite his impressive stats, the former rodeo star's leadership skills and remarkable talent were overshadowed during his career by more flamboyant players such as Ty Cobb and Babe Ruth. In his 1995 biography of Speaker, author Timothy Gay shed new light on this largely forgotten Hall of Famer, extolling his talent, while noting his flaws and conflicting character traits. Speaker was a member of the Ku Klux Klan, yet later served as a mentor to Larry Doby, the AL's first African-American player, and his two closest friends were both Jewish. And despite his virulent prejudices against his Irish-Catholic teammates in Boston, Speaker married an Irish-Catholic girl.

MOST TRIPLES, CAREER

312: Sam Crawford, 1899 to 1917

Born in Wahoo, Nebraska, Sam Crawford was tagged "Wahoo Sam" early in his professional career and grew so fond of the nickname that he asked that it be inscribed on his Hall of Fame plaque. Wahoo Sam was one of baseball's first power hitters, which in his day was revealed more by a player's number of triples rather than his homers. The parks were cavernous and Crawford had to leg out even the longest of his drives. In fact, 50 of his 97 career homers were inside-the-park jobs. After joining the Detroit Tigers in 1903, Crawford became a steady run producer, ranking among the AL's top 10 in RBIs every year from 1903 to 1915, and leading the circuit in 1910, 1914 and 1915. During that 13-year span he led the loop in triples five times, extra-base hits four times, and doubles, home runs and runs scored once each. However, as good as he was, for most of his career Crawford played in the very large shadow of teammate Ty Cobb. The two men never got along: Crawford resenting Cobb for replacing him as the main man in Detroit and Cobb resenting Crawford for being both a great player and a likeable person. In the end, Cobb prevailed in most baseball categories, except for career triples, where he ranks second with 295. Crawford will own this record forever. No active player has hit more than 100.

MOST RUNS BATTED IN, ONE GAME

12: Jim Bottomley, St. Louis Cardinals, September 16, 1924
12: Mark Whiten, St. Louis Cardinals, September 7, 1993

In the ninth inning of the first game of a 1993 doubleheader against
the Cincinnati Reds, outfielder Mark Whiten misplayed Reggie Sanders' liner into a two-run triple that gave the Reds a 14–13 win. But the
26 year old redeemed himself in the second game at Riverfront Stadium with a hitting display for the ages. Whiten drove in 12 runs in a
15–2 Cardinals' victory, cracking a grand slam, two three-run homers
and a two-run homer. Thirteen other players, including such titans as
Lou Gehrig, Willie Mays, Gil Hodges and Mike Schmidt, have dialed
long distance four times in one game, but none of them ever collected
12 RBIs. Counting the one RBI that Whiten picked up in the first game
of the twin bill, he also tied the record of 13 RBIs in a doubleheader,
set by San Diego's Nate Colbert in 1972. Amazingly, Whiten's dozen
RBIs did not set a stand-alone Cardinals franchise record. On September 16, 1924, another Cardinal, "Sunny Jim" Bottomley, drove in 12
runs against the Brooklyn Dodgers during a 17–3 St. Louis triumph at
Ebbets Field. The first baseman and future Hall of Famer went six-for-
six at the plate, with a double, two home runs and three runs scored.

AGE OF YOUNGEST PLAYER TO HIT 500 HOME RUNS

32 years, eight days: Alex Rodriguez, August 4, 2007

At last count, the 500-home-run club had only 25 members, making it one of baseball's most prestigious fraternities. Most players reached the plateau late in their careers: Mickey Mantle and Mark McGwire were 35 when they joined the club, Barry Bonds was 36, while Ted Williams was 41. Only two sluggers cracked the milestone before their 33rd birthdays: Jimmy Foxx and Alex Rodriguez. Foxx made it to 500 homers at 32 years and 336 days, but he then went into a rapid decline and hit only 42 more homers before retiring five years later. Rodriguez bettered Foxx's mark by 328 days when he blasted a pitch by Royals hurler Kyle Davies into the left-field seats at Yankee Stadium for a three-run homer on August 4, 2007. He had waited eight days and 28 at-bats for the envisioned achievement to become a reality. When the ball fell into a pack of frenzied fans, Rodriguez raised his hands in the air, accepting congratulations from first-base coach Tony Pena before clapping and grinning as he rounded the bases. The zillionaire third baseman now looks to have a decent shot at overtaking Bonds as baseball's all-time home-run champ. At even 75 percent of his current rate, A-Rod would reach 760 homers during the 2014 season—which he would start as a 38-year-old. At that age, Bonds had amassed only 567 homers.

78

AGE OF THE YOUNGEST PLAYER TO WIN THE MVP AWARD

22 years, 62 days: Vida Blue, Oakland Athletics, 1971

Vida Blue hit the American League like a bolt of lightning. After two brief call-ups in previous years, Blue joined Oakland's starting rotation for good in 1971. He lost his first start, then reeled off 10 straight wins, all complete games in which he allowed six hits or less; five of them shutouts. When the All-Star Game rolled around, the southpaw had 17 wins and just three losses and was baseball's biggest gate attraction. Blue possessed a curveball that he threw on occasion and a decent changeup, but his signature pitch was a blistering fastball that dialed up to nearly 100 mph. Asked to describe Blue's hummer, Roy White of the Yankees said "it speeds up on you and then seems to disappear." After his world champion Baltimore Orioles were humiliated by Blue in two straight games, scoring only one run in 18 innings, manager Earl Weaver griped, "Our guys just didn't see the damn ball." Blue finished his first full season in the majors with a 24–8 record, 301 strikeouts and a 1.82 ERA. He led the Athletics to their first World Series since 1931 and won the AL MVP Award and the Cy Young. It's hard to imagine how any pitcher could top that, and Blue didn't. Although he posted two more 20-win seasons and played on three World Series champions, Blue developed drug-addiction problems and never fanned more than 189 batters again, ending his career with a 209–161 record.

79

HIGHEST WINNING PERCENTAGE BY A PITCHER, ONE SEASON

.947: Elroy Face, Pittsburgh Pirates, 1959

Elroy Face is a forgotten figure in baseball's pantheon, but he is a pivotal player in several respects. He was the first hurler to achieve success as a closer and he also was the first to master the forkball, the forerunner of today's split-finger fastball. Face stood only five foot eight, wore false teeth and had a perpetually mournful expression, but he threw hard, putting so much oomph into his pitches that all 155 pounds of him quivered, as one teammate noted, "like a little ol' wet mouse shaking itself dry." In 1959, Face went 18–1, to set records for most wins by a reliever and for the highest single-season winning percentage by a pitcher. He won 17 of those games consecutively, which, when combined with the five straight that he won in 1958, gave him 22 in a row, just two behind Carl Hubbell's record of 24 consecutive victories. Face's bid for that record ended when the Dodgers beat him and the Bucs 5–4 on September 11. Despite his dazzling numbers, Face may have actually been more effective in 1958 and 1960. He blew nine of 19 save opportunities in 1959; four of those resulted in wins when Pittsburgh rallied late. The year before when his win-loss record was 5–2, he saved 20 of 21 chances and blew only two games. In 1960, he saved 24 of 26 opportunities and blew only five games. Luck, and the Pirates' timely hitting had a lot to do with creating Face's charmed season.

MOST CONSECUTIVE GAMES WITHOUT BEING SHUT OUT

308: New York Yankees, August 3, 1931 to August 2, 1933

Led by the booming bats of Babe Ruth and Lou Gehrig, the New York Yankees terrorized the American League in 1931, scoring a record 1,067 runs and sending a steady parade of opposing pitchers to the showers. New York was blanked only twice that season, 4–0 by Philadephia's George Earnshaw on May 1, and 1–0 by Boston's Wilcy Moore on August 2, in the second game of a doubleheader played at Braves Field, the home of Boston's NL club. The game had been moved from Fenway Park because the stadium was located near a church, violating the city's Sunday Blue Laws. The Bronx Bombers were not whitewashed again until August 3, 1933, a span of 308 games, or, as measured back then, exactly two seasons. The streak came to a jarring halt at Yankee Stadium when Lefty Grove and the Philadelphia Athletics spanked the Yanks 7–0. Admittedly, shutouts were not as common an occurrence in the early 1930s as they were in other eras, but even so, no other team has come anywhere close to matching this astounding skein. The next longest streak (212 games) was compiled by the AL's Milwaukee Brewers between 1978 and 1979. The NL standard belongs to the Cincinnati Reds, who went 208 games without being blanked between April 3, 2000 and May 23, 2001.

MOST GRAND SLAMS, CAREER

23: Lou Gehrig, 1923 to 1939

Had Lou Gehrig not played for America's glamor team, the New York Yankees, he would not be as famous as he is. By the same token, if Gehrig had not suited up alongside Babe Ruth for so much of his career, his baseball talents would be better appreciated. When asked by historian Fred Lieb about playing in Ruth's shadow, Gehrig replied, "It's a pretty big shadow, it gives me lots of room to spread myself. Let's face it, I'm not a headline guy. I always knew that as long as I was following Babe to the plate I could have gone up there and stood on my head. No one would have noticed the difference." In 1927, the season that Gehrig won the MVP Award by batting .373 with 52 doubles, 20 triples, 47 home runs and 175 RBIs, Ruth clobbered a record 60 homers. Ruth earned $70,000 that year; Gehrig made $7,500. Gehrig never emerged from that shadow. Only after Babe's career was winding down did he claim a home-run title outright, with 49 in 1934. When Gehrig batted .545 in the 1928 World Series, Ruth hit .625. However, one department that Ruth did not outpace Gehrig in was career grand slams. The Iron Horse belted a major-league record 23 compared to Ruth's 16. Unlike Gehrig's consecutive-games streak, this mark still stands, though Manny Ramirez, who had 21 slams entering 2010, may still break it.

MOST ASSISTS BY A SHORTSTOP, ONE SEASON

621: Ozzie Smith, San Diego Padres, 1980

Shortstop is considered the most athletically demanding position in baseball, and no one was more athletic than Ozzie Smith. As New York Mets shortstop Bud Harrelson said about Smith: "The thing about Ozzie is, if he misses a ball, you assume it's uncatchable. If any other shortstop misses a ball, your first thought is, 'Would Ozzie have had it?'" Known for his acrobatic style and trademark, pre-game backflip, Smith won his first of 13 consecutive Gold Glove Awards with San Diego in 1980, the same year he set the single-season record for assists by a shortstop with 621. Smith also led all shortstops in total chances, putouts and double plays. After the 1981 season, in which he was named to his first of 12 straight All-Star teams, Smith was traded to the Cardinals for shortstop Garry Templeton. At the time it seemed the Padres had gotten the better of the deal, as Templeton was a far superior hitter. But after switching cities, the two saw their careers head in opposite directions. Smith learned to hit, while Templeton's knee injuries prevented him from maintaining the high level of performance that defined his early career. Meanwhile, The Wizard of Oz led NL shortstops in fielding percentage nine times, assists eight times, double plays five times and range factor eight times.

MOST GAMES PLAYED, CAREER

3,562: Pete Rose, 1963 to 1986

Pete Rose once memorably declared, "I'd walk through hell in a gas-oline suit to play baseball." The man they called Charlie Hustle not only played more games than anyone in major-league history, he did it while playing more than 500 games at each of five different positions: left field, right field, third base, second base and first base. Versatile is just one of the many adjectives to describe Rose, who was also one of the most competitive, combative and energetic players to appear on a baseball diamond. Even after being walked, Rose would sprint to first, instead of the traditional trot to the bag. He also became famous for recklessly sliding headfirst into a base, a method since copied by a legion of base stealers. Rose is vividly remembered for bowling over catcher Ray Fosse in a home-plate collision at the 1970 All-Star Game. Fosse, who suffered a separated shoulder from the impact, was never the same player afterwards. Three years later, during Game 3 of the National League Championship Series, Rose got into a fight with New York Mets shortstop Bud Harrelson while trying to break up a double play, igniting a bench-clearing brawl. All told, the hard-charging Rose played in 150 games or more in 17 seasons, two seasons more than iron-man Cal Ripken Jr., and participated in a record 1,972 winning games.

MOST HOME RUNS, ONE WORLD SERIES

5: Reggie Jackson, New York Yankees, 1977
5: Chase Utley, Philadelphia Phillies, 2009

Have two record holders ever been so different? Other than the fact that both Chase Utley and Reggie Jackson swing from the left side, the two players could inhabit parallel universes. Jackson was one of the most lethal power hitters of his era, a muscular free-swinger who would often twist himself into the ground if he failed to make contact. "Mr. October" was also gregarious, egotistical and obsessed with the spotlight. Utley, a slim second baseman with a quick, compact swing, has never hit more than 33 home runs in a season, dislikes publicity, shuns interviews and plays with a business-like demeanor. So it was not surprising that after Utley took Yankees reliever Phil Coke deep in Game 5 of the 2009 World Series to tie Jackson's record, he blitzed around the bases with his head down as if he were being chased. The scene was far different in 1977, when Jackson, who had already drilled homers in Game 4 and 5 of the Series, earned himself a place in baseball lore by slamming three bombs into the seats in Game 6, each on the first pitch he saw, off three different Los Angeles Dodger pitchers. The Yankees won the game 8–4 to take the title and Jackson was voted Series MVP. Utley's five dingers put him in the record book, but left no dramatic impression, as his team lost Game 6 and the Series to the Yankees.

HIGHEST PERCENTAGE OF A TEAM'S WINS, ONE SEASON

45.8: Steve Carlton, Philadelphia Phillies, 1972

After becoming embroiled in a salary dispute with Steve Carlton prior
to the 1972 season, St. Louis Cardinals owner Gussie Busch ordered
the big lefty to be traded. He was quickly dispatched to the Phillies for
pitcher Rick Wise. The transaction is now considered one of the worst
trades in Cardinals history. Carlton went on to win four Cy Young
Awards in the City of Brotherly Love, but his most stunning was his first
in 1972. Despite toiling for the cellar-dwelling Phils, a team that managed to win only 59 games, he chalked up a league-high 27 victories
to equal the NL record for southpaws set by Sandy Koufax in 1966. He
also topped the NL with 30 complete games, 346 innings, 310 strikeouts
and a 1.97 ERA. Incredibly, none of the other starters on this offensively
challenged team won more than four games. Still, Carlton flourished
with little to no run support and a bullpen that was shaky at best. Not
only was he the first pitcher from a last-place team to lead his league in
wins, his 27 victories represented 45.8 percent of the Phillies' total, a
20th-century record. Carlton attributed his success to his grueling training regime, which included various Eastern martial arts techniques, the
most famous of which was repeatedly twisting his fist to the bottom of a
five-gallon bucket of rice.

MOST POSTSEASON SAVES, CAREER

39. Mariano Rivera, 1995 to 2009

"Enter Sandman" by Metallica, a song about an evil entity who gives children nightmares, plays each time that Mariano Rivera jogs in from the bullpen. The Sandman is a fantasy figure, but Rivera is very real, and so are the nightmares that he induces in hitters with his lethal cutter. The pitch, which the Panamanian routinely throws at about 93 mph, breaks sharply away from right-hand hitters and in toward left-hand hitters, moving as much as six inches. Left-handers find his cutter especially tough to deal with as it darts suddenly in on their hands. Atlanta's Chipper Jones once likened the pitch to a "buzz saw" after watching teammate Ryan Klesko break three bats in a plate appearance against Rivera in the 1999 World Series. Working with the cool composure of an assassin, Rivera has closed the door on opposing teams more than 500 times in his career. Entering the 2010 season, he sported a postseason record of 8–1 and a WHIP of 0.77, and held numerous postseason records, including lowest ERA (0.74), most saves (39) and most consecutive scoreless innings pitched in a World Series (34⅓). Trevor Hoffman, the only man with more regular-season career saves than Rivera, said about the Yankee closer, "He will go down as the best reliever in history. His presence in the postseason is so strong that the other team knows that if they're losing in the eighth inning, they are going to lose."

MOST SHUTOUTS BY A PITCHER, ONE WORLD SERIES

3: Christy Mathewson, New York Giants, 1905

If Christy Mathewson didn't exist, baseball would have had to invent him. At a time when the game was awash with uncouth, hard-drinking roughnecks, Mathewson was a Bucknell graduate who headed two college literary societies, sang for the campus choir and was a champion in everything from football to checkers. Later in his life, he also wrote a series of children's books. Handsome and wholesome, Mathewson is personally credited with attracting women and entire families to New York's Polo Grounds. The man they called "Big Six" was also the greatest pitcher of the era. Employing a good fastball, a wicked curveball, a pitch he called the "fadeaway" (now known as the "screwball") and superb control, he posted 2,502 career strikeouts and only 844 walks. Between 1903 and 1914, his *lowest* victory total was 22. Four times he topped the 30-win mark and five times he led the NL in strikeouts. Mathewson's heroics against the Philadelphia Athletics in the 1905 World Series sealed his legend. In Game 1, Mathewson threw a four-hit shutout in a 3–0 win. Three days later, with the series tied 1–1, he fashioned another four-hit shutout as the Giants won 9–0. Then, pitching on just one day's rest, he tossed a five-hit shutout in Game 5 as the Giants beat the A's 2–0 to take the Series.

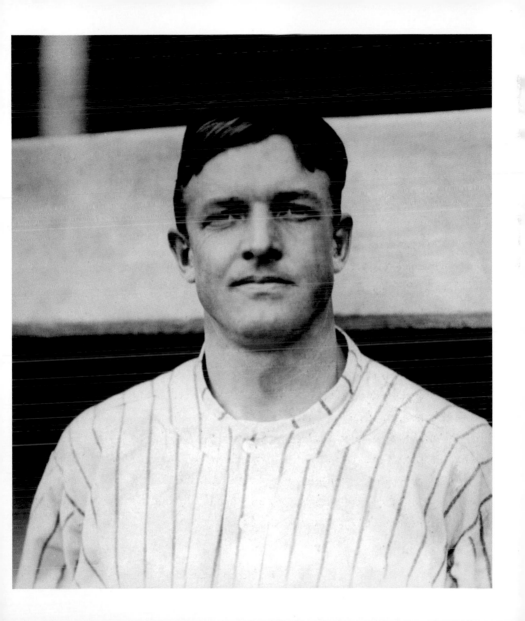

MOST HOME RUNS BY A ROOKIE, ONE SEASON

49: Mark McGwire, Oakland Athletics, 1987

Before he bulked up to 250 pounds with performance-enhancing substances and dedicated gym work, Mark McGwire could still belt the ball. The six-foot-five native of Pomona, California, proved this in his rookie campaign, when, despite weighing a mere 200 pounds, he blasted 49 homers, obliterating the majors' record of 38, held jointly by Frank Robinson and Wally Berger, and tying Chicago Cubs outfielder Andre Dawson for the most four-baggers in the majors. As a result of his hitting exploits, McGwire was the unanimous choice as the 1987 AL Rookie of the Year. The hard-swinging first baseman then clubbed 32, 33 and 39 homers in the next three seasons with Oakland, to become the first major leaguer to hit 30 or more home runs in each of his first four full seasons. A string of nagging ailments and a hitting slump slowed him down in the early 1990s, but by 1995 he was suddenly bigger and stronger and knocking the ball out of the park once again. In 1996, McGwire led the majors in dingers, when he went deep 52 times, the first of four straight seasons in which he topped all players. After his July 1997 trade to St. Louis, McGwire became one of baseball's biggest attractions, and in 1998 his back-and-forth home-run contest with Sammy Sosa to break Roger Maris's single-season record of 61 made him a national celebrity.

MOST DOUBLES, ONE SEASON

67: Earl Webb, Boston Red Sox, 1931

Earl Webb was a shy kid from a Tennessee coal-mining community who spent several years shuffling through the minors before graduating to the big time with the New York Giants in 1925. However, Webb achieved no success until he was acquired by the Boston Red Sox in 1930. In his second season in Beantown, the right fielder somehow managed to bang out a record 67 doubles. No one else in history has ever hit more than 64, and since 1893 only five other players have hit as many as 60. When Boston manager Shano Collins was asked why Webb rang up so many two-baggers in 1931, Collins replied, "He hits a long, hard ball and he's too darned slow on the bases to get to third." But this answer fails to explain why Webb never managed to hit more than 30 doubles in any other of his five major-league seasons. (And the left-handed hitting Webb did not benefit from rapping liners off Fenway Park's famed Green Monster, as the wall was not erected in left field until 1934). For whatever reason, Webb got off to a fast start in 1931. He was batting .371 through July, but then slumped, hitting .270 the rest of the way to finish with a .333 average. Reportedly, at some point in August, Webb accidentally put iodine in one of his eyes, an incident that may have contributed to his second-half struggles. Webb's hitting tailed off after 1931, and he was done by 1933, having posted a .306 average in 650 games.

MOST DOUBLE PLAYS BY A SECOND BASEMAN, ONE SEASON

161: Bill Mazeroski, Pittsburgh Pirates, 1966

Total Baseball, the official encyclopedia of Major League Baseball, ranks Bill Mazeroski as the best defensive second baseman of all time. Baseball analyst Bill James goes even further, stating, "Mazeroski's defensive statistics are probably the most impressive of any player at any position." Mazeroski won eight Gold Gloves and made six All-Star squads, led all NL second basemen in fielding percentage three times and topped the league five times in putouts, in chances accepted a record eight times, nine times in assists and eight times in double plays. Teaming with shortstop Gene Alley, the tobacco-chewing West Virginian turned 161 double plays in 1966, the record for a second baseman in a single season, as the Pirates set an NL record with 215 twin-killings. He also holds the majors' lifetime mark with 1,706 double plays. To give you an idea of how dominant Mazeroski was during his prime, consider that during the 1960s only one other NL second basemen—the Braves' Frank Bolling—turned more than 110 double plays in a season. Mazeroski bettered that total eight times. Ironically, despite his masterful glovework, Mazeroski is best remembered for something he did with his bat—a dramatic walk-off homer in Game 7 of the 1960 World Series against the Yankees.

HIGHEST TEAM SLUGGING AVERAGE, ONE SEASON

.491: Boston Red Sox, 2003

The rallying cry for the Boston Red Sox in 2003 was "Cowboy Up," a slogan credited to first baseman Kevin Millar, who hails from Beaumont, Texas. Beaumont is in rodeo country, and in rodeo, to "cowboy up" means to hang tough in times of adversity. Millar trotted out the phrase when the media questioned the team's character after a midseason loss. "I want to see somebody cowboy up and stand behind this team and quit worrying about all the negative stuff," he growled. The Red Sox silenced their critics with a thunderous offensive display that established several major-league team records, including most extra-base hits in one season (649), most total bases in one season (2,832) and highest slugging average in one season (.491). The latter broke the long-standing milestone of .489, held by the "Murderer's Row" 1927 Yankees. Boston's potent attack featured eight players with 85 RBIs or more, led by Manny Ramirez with 37 homers and 104 RBIs, David Ortiz with 31 homers and 101 RBIs and Nomar Garciaparra with 28 homers and 105 RBIs. Unfortunately for their long-suffering fans, the Red Sox's wild ride came to a heartbreaking end, when they blew a 4–0 lead in Game 7 of the American League Championship Series, eventually losing 6–5 to the Yankees in 11 innings.

MOST STRIKEOUTS BY A PITCHER, ONE WORLD SERIES GAME

17: Bob Gibson, St. Louis Cardinals, October 2, 1968

There was some debate whether St. Louis's Bob Gibson or Detroit's Denny McLain was the best pitcher in the majors in 1968. Both had posted amazing numbers: Gibson was 22–9, with 13 shutouts and a microscopic 1.12 ERA; McLain's ERA was a sterling 1.96, but even more impressive was his 31–6 win-loss record. You had to travel back to 1916 to find a pitcher who won more games. Both hurlers claimed the Cy Young and MVP in their respective leagues, so it was only fitting that the two met head-to-head in Game 1 of the World Series. McLain's team, the Tigers, had far more power, having hit a major-league-leading 185 homers, while St. Louis managed only 73. As it turned out, McLain didn't have his best stuff that day and was gone after five innings. However, Gibson did. He dominated from beginning to end, confusing and intimidating Detroit's hitters with a humming fastball and late-breaking slider. After the eighth inning, the Cardinals ace was leading 4–0 and had struck out 14 Tigers, one short of Sandy Koufax's 1963 World Series record of 15. In the ninth, he passed Koufax with style, striking out the heart of the Tigers' order—Al Kaline, Norm Cash and Willie Horton—in succession to seal the five-hit shutout. McLain would later admit, "It was the single greatest pitching performance I have ever seen."

93

MOST CONSECUTIVE STRIKEOUTS, ONE GAME

10: Tom Seaver, New York Mets, April 22, 1970

The quintessential professional, Tom Seaver won 311 games with 3,640 strikeouts and a 2.86 ERA over 20 seasons. He was the NL Rookie of the Year in 1967, a three-time Cy Young Award winner and made more Opening Day starts (16) than any pitcher in history. In his 11 years in the Big Apple from 1967 to 1977, he won 25 percent of the Mets' games. Seaver threw extremely hard; as Reggie Jackson once said, "Blind people come to the park just to listen to him pitch." But he also had pinpoint control, and his knowledge of pitching enabled him to turn to finesse when his heater was no longer overpowering. However, on April 22, 1970, Tom Terrific still had his killer stuff, as the San Diego Padres discovered. In a dominating 2–1 win at Shea Stadium, he set a major-league record by fanning the final 10 batters of the game. All told, Seaver yielded only two hits, while striking out 19. The lone run he allowed was a homer by Al Ferrara, who later became Seaver's final strikeout victim. In addition to his 10 consecutive Ks, Seaver's 19 strikeouts tied Steve Carlton's record for a nine inning game. (The mark was later eclipsed by 20-strikeout games by Kerry Wood, Randy Johnson and twice by Roger Clemens.) In 1992, Seaver was inducted into the Baseball Hall of Fame, receiving 98.8 percent of the votes, the highest percentage of all time.

AGE OF OLDEST PLAYER IN HIS MAJOR-LEAGUE DEBUT

42 years, 2 days: Satchel Paige, Cleveland Indians, 1948

"Age is a case of mind over matter," claimed Satchel Paige. "It don't matter, if you don't mind." Paige was a living advertisement for his theory. However, when Cleveland Indians owner Bill Veeck signed the 42-year-old former Negro Leagues star to a contract on July 7, 1948, the media howled in outrage. *The Sporting News* declared: "Veeck has gone too far in his quest for publicity. To sign a pitcher at Paige's age is to demean the standards of baseball." Veeck's response was telling: "If Satch were white, of course he would have been in the majors 25 years earlier and the question would not have been before the house." Although Veeck, like Paige, was a showman, this was not a publicity stunt. Veeck couldn't afford it; the Indians were locked in a tight pennant race. Paige may have been well past his prime, but he could still pitch. Manager Lou Boudreau initially used the legend only in relief, but on August 3, Paige made his first start, beating the Senators. In his next two starts, he tossed a pair of shutouts. Not only did Paige win, he brought out the crowds. More than 200,000 fans attended his first three starts, including a major-league record 78,382 for a night game, at Cleveland. Paige finished the year with a 6–1 record with one save and a 2.48 ERA, as the Indians captured the flag by one game and then went on to defeat the Boston Braves in the World Series.

HIGHEST AT-BATS-PER-STRIKEOUT RATIO, CAREER

62.6: Joe Sewell, 1920 to 1933

Joe Sewell was the personification of the term "contact hitter." The Alabama-born shortstop fanned only 114 times in 7,132 career at-bats with the Indians and Yankees, an average of one strikeout for every 62.6 at-bats. No one is even remotely close to the mark. Second is Lloyd Waner at 44.9; third is Nellie Fox at 42.7. A lifetime .312 hitter, Sewell also holds the single-season mark for fewest strikeouts over a full season, with three in 576 trips to the plate with the Yankees in 1932, as well as the record for most consecutive games without recording a strikeout, at 115. In the nine seasons from 1925 to 1933, he struck out 4, 6, 7, 9, 4, 3, 8, 3 and 4 times. According to his *New York Times* obituary, Sewell used only one bat his entire career, "Black Betsy," a 35-inch, 40-ounce Ty Cobb model Louisville Slugger, which he kept in shape by rubbing it with a Coke bottle and seasoning it with chewing tobacco. Sewell felt there were three key factors in batting: knowing the strike zone, making allowances for the umpire behind the plate and keeping your eye on the ball. "I hit the ball just about every time I swung at it," he contended. "I could see a ball leave my bat. A lot of people don't think that's possible. But it sure is. All you have to do is watch it. It doesn't disappear when you put the bat on it."

MOST CONSECUTIVE STOLEN BASES, CAREER

50: Vince Coleman, St. Louis Cardinals,
September 18, 1988 to July 26, 1989

Vince Coleman was so explosively fast that he could overcome mistakes that would have doomed other base runners. In 1987, for example, the Cardinals outfielder stole second successfully 19 consecutive times *on pitchouts.* Coleman swiped 110 bases in his debut season in 1985, easily breaking the rookie record of 72, set by the Phillies' Juan Samuel in 1984. Coleman then stole over 100 bases in each of the following two seasons as well, making him the only player in the 20th century to post three straight seasons of 100 or more steals, and the first player in history to steal 100 bases in his first three seasons. In June 1987, Coleman pilfered his 500th stolen base in just his 804th game, the fewest that any player has needed to reach that plateau, and looked destined to become the majors' all-time base thief. However after filing for free agency and leaving the Cards to sign with the New York Mets in 1990, his career went into a downward spiral. But before he left, the speed merchant raced his way into the record books by swiping 50 bases in 50 attempts, before finally being cut down by Montreal Expos catcher Nelson Santovenia. This record could be a tough one to topple, though in 2006 and 2007, Seattle's Ichiro Suzuki took a run at it, swiping 45 consecutive bases.

MOST CONSECUTIVE ERRORLESS GAMES BY A CATCHER, CAREER

252: Mike Matheny, St. Louis Cardinals,
August 2, 2002 to August 2, 2004

Unless they happen to be great hitters, catchers rarely draw much attention for their grunt work behind the plate. So it is not so surprising that Mike Matheny's amazing two-year string of errorless games with the St. Louis Cardinals has slipped completely beneath the radar. Only three backstops in major-league history have ever caught at least 100 games in a season without committing an error: Buddy Rosar of the Philadelphia Athletics in 1946 (117 games, 605 chances), Charles Johnson of the Florida Marlins in 1997 (123 games, 973 chances) and Matheny in 2003 (138 games, 823 chances). But Matheny's fielding perfection extended much longer than one season. Over a two-year span, the Cardinals catcher handled 1,555 consecutive chances without a single miscue, making 1,460 putouts and 95 assists in that time. Unfortunately, the gritty Gold-Glover, who was nicknamed "The Toughest Man Alive," had his career put in limbo in 2006 while playing for San Francisco, when he went on the disabled list after a series of foul balls caromed off his mask, resulting in a serious concussion. On February 1, 2007, Matheny announced his retirement due to on-going symptoms of post-concussion syndrome.

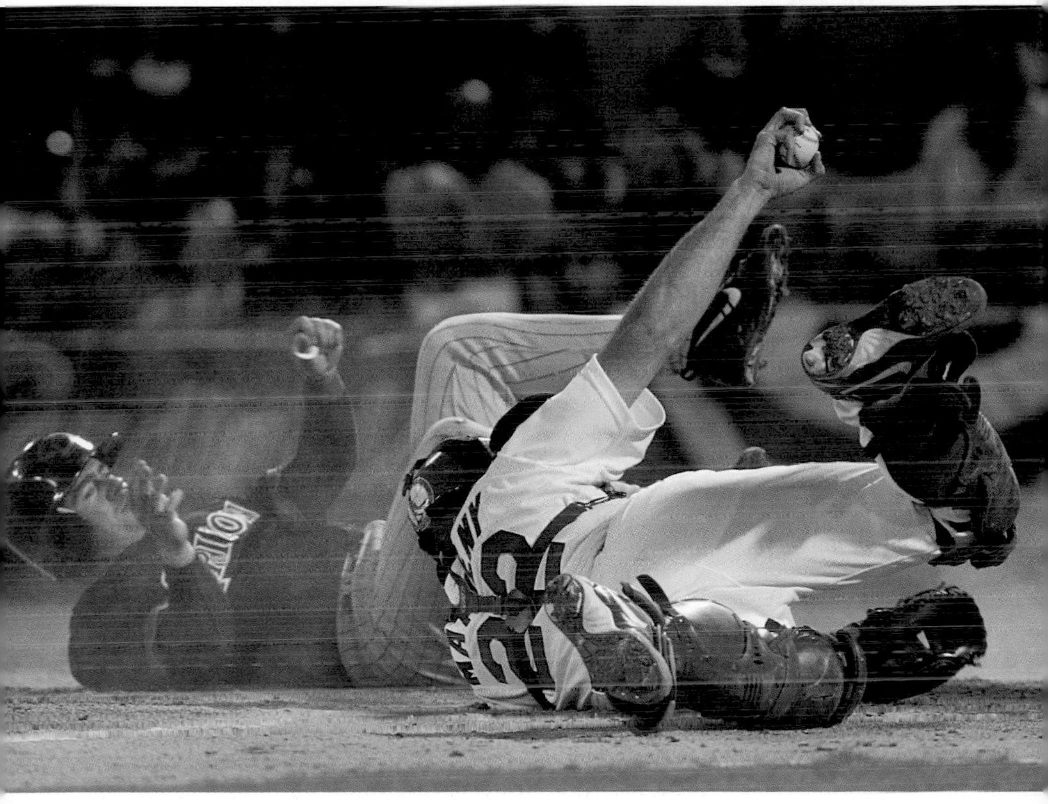

MOST GAMES PITCHED IN RELIEF, ONE SEASON

106: Mike Marshall, Los Angeles Dodgers, 1974

Mike Marshall set a record by appearing in 92 games for the Montreal Expos in 1973. The next year, with the Dodgers, the stubby, bowlegged fireman pushed the envelope even farther, appearing in 106 games and pitching a punishing 208 ⅓ innings. Marshall credited his freakish durability to his own theories on physical conditioning that he had acquired while earning a PhD in kinesiology from Michigan State University. The reliever's signature pitch was a screwball, which some would contend also described Marshall's personality. His maverick ideas and stubbornness often caused conflict with his pitching coaches. In fact, Marshall once claimed that the only pitching coach he would listen to was Isaac Newton, the physicist who developed the theory of gravity. However, no one could quarrel with his results in 1974. Sporting his distinctive muttonchop sideburns, Marshall appeared in 65 percent of the Dodgers' games, finished 83 of them, posted a 15–12 record, with 21 saves and a 2.42 ERA, and won the Cy Young Award. Today, Marshall teaches pitching at a Florida academy and maintains his own website on which he claims that he knows "the injurious flaws in the traditional baseball pitching motion that harms baseball pitchers and how to rectify these flaws and eliminate all pitching injuries."

LONGEST MAJOR-LEAGUE GAME

26 innings: Boston Braves vs. Brooklyn Robins, May 1, 1920

Incredibly, this long day's journey into night failed to produce a winner. Playing in a cold drizzle, Brooklyn took a 1–0 lead in the fifth inning when Ernie Krueger walked, advanced on a fielder's choice, then scored on Ivy Olson's single. Boston tied it in the sixth as Walt Cruise tripled and Tony Boeckel drove him in with a single. No one else would cross the plate, though both clubs had their chances. The Braves loaded the bases in the ninth with one out, but second baseman Charlie Pick, on his way to an embarrassing 0-for-11 performance, hit into an inning-ending double play. Brooklyn filled the bags in the 17th, but suffered the same fate. After 26 innings and eight hours and 22 minutes, the umpires called the game due to darkness, declaring it a 1–1 draw. There were 168 at-bats, nine walks and six sacrifices, a total of 182 batters faced. Walter Holke, the Braves first baseman, had 42 putouts. But most astounding of all was that both starting pitchers pitched the entire 26 innings! Brooklyn's Leon Cadore scattered 15 hits, walked five and struck out six. Boston's Joe Oeschger allowed only nine hits, while walking four and fanning seven. Instead of weakening, Cadore and Oeschger actually grew stronger as the game progressed: neither allowed a hit in the last six innings. After such Herculean efforts, perhaps it was fitting that neither hurler was tagged with a loss.

MOST POSTSEASON HITS, CAREER

175: Derek Jeter, 1996 to 2009

Many baseball analysts dispute the notion that certain players produce in the clutch more often than others. Derek Jeter's supporters would certainly disagree. Jeter has a reputation for coming through under pressure—Nike even named a shoe after him called the Jeter Clutch. Since he arrived in the majors in 1996, Jeter's Yankees have made the playoffs all but one year and have won seven American League Championships and five World Series titles. Jeter's teams have also won 20 of the 28 postseason series they've played in, and have compiled a remarkable postseason record of 83–42. The acrobatic shortstop has also been front and center in some memorable postseason plays, such as his miraculous out-of-nowhere grab and flip to catcher Jorge Posada, who tagged out Oakland's Jason Giambi in Game 3 of the 2001 American League Championship Series. Facing elimination, the Yankees went on to win that contest 1–0, and the series. As of 2009, Jeter was the all-time postseason leader in games played (138), runs (99), hits (175) and total bases (268). By the time he calls it quits, the Yankees' captain could conceivably put all of these marks out of reach. As it stands, he is 47 hits ahead of retired Bernie Williams and a whopping 58 hits ahead of third-ranked Manny Ramirez.

ACKNOWLEDGMENTS

Thanks to the following publications for their statistical and biographical information: *The Biographical History of Baseball*, by Donald Dewey and Nicholas Acocella, Carroll and Graf Publishers, 1995; *The SABR Baseball List and Record Book*, edited by Lyle Spatz, Scribner, 2007; *Great Baseball Feats, Facts and Firsts*, by David Nemec and Scott Flatow, New American Library, 2009 edition; *The Pitcher*, by John Thorn and John Holway, Prentice Hall, 1987; *Total Baseball*, edited by John Thorn and Pete Palmer, Warner Books, 1991 edition; *The New Bill James Historical Baseball Abstract*, by Bill James, Free Press, 2001; *The Baseball Timeline*, by Burt Solomon, Avon Books, 1997.

I am also indebted to numerous data-rich web sites, most notably www.baseball-reference.com; www.baseball-almanac.com; www.thebaseballpage.com; www.baseballlibrary.com; www.baseballhalloffame.org; www.baseball1.com; www.thebaseballcube.com; http://bioproj.sabr.org; http://baseball.suite101.com.

I also want to thank Rob Sanders and Susan Rana at Greystone Books, designers Peter Cocking and Naomi MacDougall, editor Derek Fairbridge, indexer Judith Anderson, inputter Joy Woodsworth, National Baseball Hall of Fame archivist John Horne, and photo adviser Brian Banks for their expert assistance.

PHOTO CREDITS

INDEX

Page numbers in italic indicate team or individual records.

Show, Eric, 11
Simmons, Al, 76
Simmons, Curt, 31
Simmons, Ted, 52
Sisler, George, 56
Smith, Al, 5
Smith, Eddie, 5
Smith, Ozzie, 126–27
Smoltz, John, 109
Sosa, Sammy, 78–79, 137
Spahn, Warren, 85
Span, Denard, 86
Speaker, Tris, 80, 91, 114–15
Stengel, Casey, 18, 19, 94
Suzuki, Ichiro, 46–47, 56, 147

Tatis, Fernando, 1
Taylor, Jack, 3, 28, 62
Templeton, Garry, 127
Thigpen, Bobby, 109
Tiger Stadium, 110
Toronto Blue Jays, 60

U.S. Cellular Field, 86
Utley, Chase, 130

Valenzuela, Fernando, 62
Vance, Dazzy, 43
Vander Meer, Johnny, 55
Vaughn, Greg, 69
Veeck, Bill, 145

Wagner, Honus, 3, 34, 57
Walsh, Ed, 66–67
Waner, Lloyd, 146
Waner, Paul, 57
Washington Senators, 34, 44
Weaver, Earl, 121
Webb, Earl, 3, 138
White, Roy, 121
Whiten, Mark, 117
Williams, Bernie, 106, 153
Williams, Ted, 22, 26–27, 36,
    37, 44, 45, 68, 110, 112, 118
Willis, Mike, 97
Wilson, Hack, 38–39
Wilson, Owen "Chief," 3, 57
Winfield, Dave, 31
Wise, DeWayne, 86
Wise, Rick, 131
Wood, Kerry, 84, 143

Yankee Stadium, 68, 83, 93, 97
Young, Cy, 12, 49, 89